Penguin Handbooks

The Penguin Salad Book

The Penguin

Salad Book

*Compiled by the editors of Sunset Books
and Sunset Magazine, California
Edited for Great Britain by Elizabeth Craig*

Penguin Books Ltd, Harmondsworth,
Middlesex, England
Penguin Books Inc., 7110 Ambassador Road,
Baltimore, Maryland 21207, U.S.A.
Penguin Books Australia Ltd,
Ringwood, Victoria, Australia
Penguin Books Canada Ltd, 41 Steelcase Road West,
Markham, Ontario, Canada
Penguin Books (N.Z.) Ltd, 182–190 Wairau Road,
Auckland 10, New Zealand

First published in the U.S.A. by the
Lane Book Company 1962
First published in Great Britain as a
Penguin Handbook 1965
Reprinted 1967, 1969, 1970, 1972, 1973, 1975

Copyright © Lane Book Company, 1962

Illustrations by Earl Thollander

Made and printed in Great Britain by
Cox & Wyman Ltd, London, Reading
and Fakenham
Set in Monotype Times

Contents

The Art of Salad Making

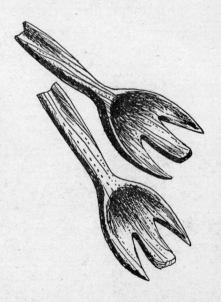

The Art of Salad Making

Now that salads have become such an important feature in our daily meals, let us do them justice. There is no mystery attached to making a perfect salad. Only imagination and care are required. The salad greens must be fresh, the dressing carefully prepared, and the garnish should blend and contrast with the greens. If you allow your imagination full rein, you may soon become famous for salads that bring new zest and excitement to your everyday meals, and add glamour to your parties.

There are many kinds of salads. You can compose a light salad or a hearty salad, a simple salad or a complex one. Some salads are suitable for serving as a first course, others as a highlight at lunch or dinner, and then there are the salads destined to accompany cold cuts or cheese. Last of all, there is the fruit salad which can be as simple or as elaborate as you please. It makes an attractive and refreshing finish to any meal.

Even the simplest of salads, however, should be prepared with infinite care and minute attention to details if it is to be a success. It must be appetizing to look at and prove a delight to the palate. Simple though it may seem, a green salad should by no means be a haphazard creation. You need fresh crisp greens, shimmering under a coat of appropriate dressing, selected to make the salad distinctive, so that it provides a suitable accompaniment to the meal with which it is to be served.

In this book you will find classic salads, variations of old favourites, and many new and unusual recipes for salads that have been created by chefs, cooks, and gourmets. They have all been thoroughly tested by experts. You will probably find many that you will want to use without changing, and others that you may wish to adapt to your own taste. Good luck!

Salads always bring variety to meals. If your own green salads have developed a rather monotonous sameness, give them new flavour accents. Try introducing unfamiliar salad greens, and use different vinegars, or combinations of vinegars, or vinegar and lemon juice, in your dressings. Let herbs, fresh or dried, transform your salads with their subtle flavour.

By changing one or two ingredients in a salad recipe, you can give it an entirely new look. Suppose, for example, you eliminate the anchovies in Caesar salad and substitute slivered salami, then you have a brand-new salad, equally exciting. If you use grated Parmesan cheese in place of blue cheese included in a salad dressing, your salad will take on an Italian look. Again, if you have a pet recipe for a chicken or turkey salad that you like to serve as a main course, you can turn it when you please into a fish salad by substituting boiled crab, lobster, or prawns for the poultry.

You will find many inspirations in this book for salads when planning party menus. Nothing could be more delicious as a first course than an attractively presented salad made of fish, coated with a tangy dressing. Arrange each on an individual plate. Imagine a shimmering moulded savoury salad, elegantly garnished, as a centrepiece at your next buffet party, or make jellied fruit the centrepiece, decorated round the base with fresh fruit and foliage.

There are many festive ways of presenting salads. For example, they look more exciting when given an attractive background. Fruits are most appealing when their rainbow colours are displayed on a handsome platter, or daintily arranged on individual plates. Use imagination when preparing and presenting fruit salads. Group colours attractively. Combine chunks of pineapple with halves of apricots, or slices of peaches or pears with berries or grapes, or fill canned half peaches or pears with fresh berries or grapes. Tuck perky sprigs of mint or watercress round the base of your fruit, or simply frame fruit with fig, strawberry, or vine leaves, or any other suitable foliage. When foliage is not available, arrange fruit on a platter covered with a gilt, plastic, or silver doiley, or in a large shallow fireproof dish, smoothly coated with silver foil.

When salads are required for a festive occasion, give them a festive setting. Use crab, lobster, or scallop shells for fish salads, and handsome shallow fluted bowls for hearty meat or poultry salads to be served as a main course. Now, serve fruit salad in attractive scalloped grapefruit or orange shells, or in shells made of halved small melons. The more dramatic the salad 'baskets' are, the more tempting the salad.

No salad of any kind is complete without a suitable garnish. It is as important to the composition of a beautiful salad as its dressing. It need not be elaborate. Sometimes all that is required for main-course salads is to serve them in a dish edged with blades of chicory, or sprigs of curly endive or watercress, or heart of lettuce leaves, and sprinkle the salad with chopped capers, chives or parsley, or paprika. To come to a green salad, garnish it with something that provides a contrast, such as wedges of hard-boiled egg or tomato, radish roses or tulips, and rings of onion or trimmed spring onions, or fluted slices of cucumber. Garnishes add a gay note to all salads. Give them special attention.

Green Salads

Green Salads

A green salad, made from crisp salad greens glistening in a coat of dressing, is an exciting addition to any meal. You can serve it with any cold savoury course as well as with cheese. Since no other type of salad is so popular as the green, it merits special consideration, for if care is not taken in its preparation the result can be disappointing.

To make a perfect green salad, first choose your salad greens. You can prepare a salad from only one kind or from a combination of several kinds which complement each other in colour, flavour, and texture. Whatever you choose must be crisp and fresh. During most of the year you have a large choice from slender dark green cos lettuce, to crisp round lettuces and leaf lettuce, curly endive, escarole, and spicy watercress. In the spring young dandelion and spinach leaves can be added to a green salad. In the summer and early autumn nasturtium leaves are an unusual addition. Basically, green salads are made of some species of lettuce, linked with other greens in season to give zest and variety to the salad.

To prepare salad greens from scratch, handle them very tenderly to prevent bruising. It is best to wash them the day before you plan to use them, so that they are crisp and chilled when required. Wash them quickly but thoroughly in running cold water, then remove any wilted leaves, but if preparing lettuce with hearts, sometimes called 'heads', do not separate the leaves. Stand this type of lettuce upside down on a rack and leave it to drain for 30 minutes. Shake off any remaining moisture from washed salad greens by gently tossing them in a clean towel, or by shaking them gently in a lettuce basket. Now place greens in the section of your refrigerator provided for crisping salads, or chill in a plastic bag in refrigerator. When required for dressing, gently pat off any moisture left on the leaves with a dry cloth, then tear into bite-size pieces. (If you are making a green salad for a large party, you can tear the leaves an hour ahead and store them loosely in large plastic bags in the refrigerator.)

The most popular dressing for a green salad is the true French type, usually made of three parts oil to one part vinegar or lemon juice, or to half part vinegar and half part lemon juice. This is the basic formula, but you can change it according to taste. One way is to vary the vinegars used in making the dressing. Cider, malt, and wine are most popular, but sometimes a little tarragon vinegar is included. Some people like dressings flavoured with celery salt, curry powder, paprika, Tabasco, or Worcester sauce. Others insist on the addition of a little sugar or French mustard. You can add individuality to some green salads by making a special dressing with a strong character of its own. The Caesar salad and the Green Goddess (on pages 21 and 26) are examples of a green salad that features an unusual dressing. No matter the constituents of a dressing, it must be seasoned with freshly ground black pepper to give it the zest and zip that it needs, so treat yourself to a pepper mill for grinding the pepper corns if you have not already got one.

Strictly speaking, a green salad should consist only of green saladings, tossed in a carefully seasoned dressing. If you add other ingredients, regard them merely as accessories. Never let them predominate. Some additions that have special value because of flavour or texture are capers, mixed herbs, green, ripe, or stuffed olives, and caraway seeds. Either toss them with the salad or sprinkle them on top.

To give a green salad a seasonal touch, fruit, or vegetables, either raw or cooked, may be added. The list is endless. Some of the most popular additions are diced avocado pear, chopped green pepper, or rings of green pepper, rings of onion, radish roses or tulips, and slices or wedges of tomato. For more unusual additions, choose between slightly cooked asparagus tips, grated raw beetroot, sliced raw or cooked mushrooms, seedless grapes, and slices of apple dipped in grapefruit or lemon juice.

1. Green Salad, Smörgåsbord Style

Here is a Continental way of serving a green salad at a party. Place the salad greens, dressing, and accompaniments on the table or buffet in separate containers. Just before the meal, or when it is time to serve the salad, the host or hostess should add the dressing to the salad greens and toss the mixture with a wooden salad fork and spoon until the leaves are evenly coated, then serve it in individual salad bowls or plates and pass them to the guests or the guests help themselves. The accompaniments vary according to the season and shopping facilities. Here are some that are popular. Halved canned artichoke hearts, either preserved in oil or pickled, avocado cubes, slices of beetroot, quartered hard-boiled eggs, freshly sliced mushrooms, stoned olives stuffed with tiny sticks of cheese, onion rings, trimmed radishes, and crumbled crisply fried bacon mixed with halved toasted cashew nuts or filberts.

When preparing a salad in this way, you can use any selection of salad greens that will result in a colourful salad full of flavour. It is a good idea to combine different types of lettuce with curly endive or chicory to give you a good balance of texture. Some salads are improved by garnishing with fried croûtons, grated Parmesan cheese, or thin lemon curls.

In brief, to make a success of this type of salad, take the crisp cold salad greens to the table or buffet in a large salad bowl and other ingredients in small wooden or fancy bowls, such as Chinese rice bowls, or even in finger bowls, or in large wine glasses. The more decorative the containers, the more attractive will the service be.

2. Basic Green Salad

Wash a head of leafy lettuce, or an assortment of salad greens, gently and quickly in cold water. Shake very well, then carefully pat dry with a cloth or paper towels. Place in a plastic bag or in the crisping compartment of refrigerator and chill. When required, tear salad greens into bite-size pieces and place in a bowl.

Put a teaspoon of salt in the bottom of a large wooden salad bowl. Peel a clove of garlic. (A fresh clove of garlic will peel easily after it is hit briskly with a knife handle.) Now hold the garlic between your thumb and forefinger and grind it on the salt until half the clove is gone. Discard the remainder. Add a sprinkling of flavouring, crushed or minced herbs, and then the salad greens. Sprinkle with two tablespoons olive oil. Toss gently until all the leaves are coated, then grind black pepper over to taste. Stir in two teaspoons wine vinegar. Toss lightly. Makes about four servings.

3. Spinach and Egg Salad

1 hard-boiled egg
1 peeled clove garlic
¼ teaspoon each dry mustard and pepper
½ teaspoon paprika
1 teaspoon salt
½ gill vinegar
¼ pint salad oil
2 tablespoons chopped parsley
1 small onion, thinly sliced
¼ lb. fresh young spinach
1 medium-sized lettuce

Crisp, dark green, slightly spicy spinach gives lettuce a sharp accent in this salad dressed with vinegar, oil, and well-selected seasonings. Thinly sliced spring onions could be substituted for the onion, if liked.

Separate egg yolk from white and drop egg yolk into a salad bowl which has been rubbed with the cut clove of garlic. Mash yolk with a wooden spoon. Add the seasonings, then stir in the vinegar and oil. Chop egg white and mix in with the parsley. Add sliced onion and the raw spinach and lettuce which have been torn into bite-size pieces. Toss lightly. Makes 4 or 5 servings.

4. Frosted Lettuce Wedges

1 teaspoon chilli powder
½ teaspoon water
½ pint mayonnaise
1 can (6 oz.) tomato paste
1 teaspoon garlic salt
2 medium-sized lettuces

Garlic salt picks up the individual flavours in the creamy dressing that frosts these lettuce wedges.

Dissolve chilli powder in water, then stir into mayonnaise along with tomato paste and garlic salt. Beat until smooth, then let stand 30 minutes. Cut each lettuce in 4 wedges. Frost with dressing just before serving. Makes 8 servings.

5. Spinach and Tomato Salad

Tear 1 small bunch of spinach into small pieces. Halve about 10 cherry tomatoes. Mix with the spinach. Toss with French dressing just before serving. Makes 3 servings.

6. Lemon Lettuce

½ gill lemon juice
2 teaspoons sugar
1 small head of lettuce

Lemon and sugar make a good dressing for a lettuce salad to be served with cold fish or game.

Pour lemon juice over sugar and let stand 2 hours. Stir mixture occasionally so it becomes syrupy. Trim lettuce, remove core, then tear into chunks or cut into wedges. Spoon lemon dressing over lettuce just before serving. Makes 4 servings.

7. Fascination Salad

8 slices bacon, cut into ½-inch pieces
1 medium-sized head of lettuce
½ gill chopped spring onion (including some of the tops)
2 hard-boiled eggs, sliced

The fascinating thing about this salad is that in spite of the hot bacon-flavoured dressing, the lettuce retains its crispness.

Fry the bacon until crisp and browned. Drain, and use the drippings in making the dressing. Break lettuce into bite-size pieces in a salad bowl. Add spring onion and egg slices. Pour over the bacon dressing, tossing lightly. Serve immediately. Makes 6 to 8 servings.

BACON DRESSING:
Measure ½ gill of the bacon drippings, and put back into frying pan. Add 3 tablespoons vinegar or lemon juice; 1 teaspoon sugar; ½ teaspoon *each* paprika, dry mustard, and salt; and a dash of pepper. Stir over low heat until hot.

8. Green Salad with Cucumber and Buttermilk Dressing

4 tablespoons buttermilk
2 tablespoons mayonnaise
2 tablespoons lemon juice
¼ teaspoon dill seed
¼ teaspoon salt
Freshly ground pepper
¼ cucumber (about a 4-inch section), finely diced
4 to 6 cups shredded crisp lettuce

Shake all ingredients together except lettuce. Pour over lettuce and toss lightly. Makes 4 to 6 servings.

9. Egg and Olive Lettuce Salad

1 head lettuce
2 hard-boiled eggs
2 tablespoons chopped ripe olives
2 tablespoons diced green pepper
1 tablespoon finely cut chives
1½ gills salad oil
½ gill mild vinegar or lemon juice
½ tablespoon sugar
1 teaspoon each salt, paprika, and dry mustard
¼ teaspoon pepper
Finely minced onion or garlic to taste

Break lettuce into bite-size pieces in a salad bowl. Press eggs through a fine sieve. Add eggs, olives, green pepper, and chives to lettuce. To make dressing, combine remaining ingredients and shake or mix well. Add dressing to taste. Toss lightly and serve. Makes 4 or 5 servings.

10. Spinach Greens Salad with Nut Dressing

¼ cup chopped pine nuts*
½ gill salad or olive oil
3 tablespoons tarragon vinegar
¼ teaspoon grated lemon peel
½ teaspoon salt
Dash nutmeg
2½ pints torn fresh spinach
* When not available, substitute cashew nuts or pecans.

Combine nuts, salad or olive oil, vinegar, lemon peel, salt, and nutmeg.
Toss with spinach. Makes 6 servings.

11. Creamy Lettuce Salad

3 small heads of lettuce
   or 3 pints of leaf lettuce
6 rashers bacon
1 tablespoon flour
¼ pint soured cream
2 tablespoons vinegar
2 teaspoons caster sugar
1 teaspoon salt

For luncheon you might serve this salad with rye or wholemeal bread
and cheese sandwiches. As a dinner salad, its flavour would go well with
steak, lamb chops, or fried chicken.

Wash the lettuce and drain well. Break into a large salad bowl. Cut the
bacon into small pieces and fry until crisp and browned. Add flour to
the bacon and drippings, and stir over low heat until flour is well blended.
Add soured cream, vinegar, sugar, and salt. Stir constantly until mixture
is a smooth, thin sauce. Pour over the lettuce. Toss lightly and serve at
once. Makes 6 to 8 servings when used as a dinner salad, or 5 to 6 when
offered at luncheon.

12. Spanish Salad

1 large peeled clove of garlic
3 slices French bread, toasted
3 hard-boiled eggs
1 head of lettuce or a cos lettuce
½ cup minced ripe olives
French dressing or mayonnaise

Rub garlic on slices of toasted French bread. Cut toast into small cubes or tear into small pieces. Chop eggs finely, tear lettuce into bite-size pieces. Combine toast cubes, chopped eggs, minced olives, and lettuce, and toss with French dressing or mayonnaise. Makes 6 servings.

13. Spinach and Bacon Salad

2 lb. fresh spinach
2 hearts leaf lettuce
*   or 1 heart iceberg lettuce*
¼ lb. bacon
1 oz. caster sugar
1 teaspoon each salt and dry
*   mustard*
1 tablespoon juice scraped from
*   onion*
4 tablespoons cider vinegar
¼ pint salad oil
1 tablespoon poppy seed (optional)
¾ lb. large curd cottage cheese

I recommend this crisp, green salad for both its flavour and its appearance. The thin, tangy dressing is slightly sweet, so you may prefer to serve the salad Continental style, as a separate course after the meat.

Thoroughly wash and drain the spinach. Break off stems and tear apart large leaves. Combine with the lettuce, torn in bite-size pieces. Fry bacon until crisp, then cool, crumble and add to salad greens. For the dressing, combine the sugar, salt, mustard, onion juice, vinegar, and salad oil. Shake or beat well. Add poppy seeds, if used, and shake again. Use about half of this dressing to dress the salad. Add cottage cheese to remaining dressing. Toss with salad greens. Makes 8 servings.

14. Stuffed Hearts of Lettuce

Select 2 medium-sized, well-formed hearts of iceberg lettuce (they should be green and rather loose). Remove loose outer leaves and the core. Run cold water into core to loosen head; drain very thoroughly. Make dressing by whirling in a blender or electric mixer, until smooth, ½ pint each soured cream and mayonnaise and 4–5 oz. crumbled blue cheese, according to taste. Slowly pour dressing into cored part and between leaves of lettuce heads, so lettuce absorbs as much dressing as possible. Wrap heads in waxed paper or clean, damp towels. Chill in vegetable compartment of refrigerator 6 hours or until dressing is firm. Cut heads in quarter wedges. Serve immediately. Makes 8 servings.

NOTE : If no electric blender or mixer is available, use a rotary egg-beater.

15. Caesar Salad

1 peeled clove garlic
1½ gills olive oil or salad oil
2 cups croûtons
2 large cos lettuces
¼ teaspoon salt
Freshly ground pepper
2 eggs, boiled for 1 minute
Juice of 1 large lemon
6 to 8 anchovy fillets, chopped
2 oz. grated Parmesan cheese

Caesar Salad is invariably dressed at the table, where everyone can watch the host or hostess season and mix the salad greens and drop in each additional ingredient – eggs, anchovies, cheese, and croûtons – with a flourish.

Crush garlic in a small bowl. Pour in the oil, and let stand several hours. Brown the croûtons (preferably made from stale French bread) in ½ gill of the garlic oil, stirring often. (If you prefer, you can toast the bread cubes in a slow oven.) Tear lettuce into a large salad bowl. Sprinkle with salt, and grind in a generous amount of pepper. Pour in remaining garlic oil and toss until every leaf is glossy.

Break the eggs into salad. Squeeze in the lemon juice, and toss thoroughly. Add chopped anchovy fillets and grated cheese, and toss again. Lastly, add the croûtons, toss gently, and serve immediately. Makes about 12 servings.

16. Syrian Spinach Salad

1 lb. fresh young spinach
1 teaspoon salt
4 spring onions, finely sliced
2 tablespoons each lemon juice
*   and olive oil*
¼ cup (⅛ pint) chopped salted nuts

Chopped salted pecans, when available, give a totally new character to raw spinach salad, dressed simply with lemon juice and olive oil. Cashew nuts may also be used.

Wash spinach thoroughly and cut off coarse stems and roots. Drain well and shake to remove excess moisture. Chop coarsely and turn into a shallow pan. Sprinkle with salt and roll and toss spinach in your hands, then squeeze dry. Turn into a salad bowl. Add onions, lemon juice, and olive oil, and toss lightly. Sprinkle with nuts. Makes 4 servings.

17. Summer Salad

2 cups finely sliced fresh spinach
1½ cups sliced peeled cucumbers
4 tablespoons sliced spring
*   onion including some of the tops*
½ cup sliced radishes
1 pint creamed cottage cheese
½ pint soured cream
2 teaspoons lemon juice
½ teaspoon salt
Freshly ground pepper
Parsley and paprika for garnish

This crisp green salad makes an ideal first course for lunch or dinner on a hot day. Serve it with crisp toast, or French bread, and butter.

In a bowl combine sliced spinach, sliced cucumbers, onions, and radishes. Toss together lightly. Arrange on 4 individual salad plates or in wooden salad bowls. In centre of each serving, place a mound of cottage cheese. Blend together soured cream, with lemon juice, salt, and pepper, and pour over salads. Sprinkle top of each salad with a little paprika and chopped parsley. Makes 4 servings.

18. Chef's Salad

4 to 6 rashers bacon
4 to 6 cups torn salad greens
3 hard-boiled eggs
¼ lb. shredded cooked ham
3 spring onions and tops
½ gill vinegar
1 teaspoon caster sugar
Salt and pepper
Worcester Sauce
2 tablespoons chopped ripe olives

You would be right to call this either a chef's salad or a wilted lettuce salad – it borrows ideas from both.

Cook bacon until crisp. Drain. Save 4 tablespoons bacon drippings in pan. Place greens in salad bowl. Chop eggs. Arrange on greens with ham. Slice onions and sauté in drippings. Add vinegar and sugar. Add salt, Worcester sauce, and pepper to taste. Pour hot dressing over greens. Crumble bacon on top. Sprinkle with the chopped ripe olives, and toss. Makes 6 servings.

19. Orange and Cucumber Green Salad

3 large oranges
1 small cucumber
2 heads lettuce
½ mild onion
DRESSING:
¼ pint salad oil
3 tablespoons wine vinegar
¼ teaspoon chilli powder
Salt and freshly ground pepper to taste

Peel and slice oranges. Remove all membrane. Slice cucumbers, peeled if desired. Thinly slice onion and separate into rings. Arrange whole leaves of lettuce in a large, shallow salad bowl. Tuck orange slices and cucumber slices among the lettuce leaves. Arrange onion rings in over-lapping circles on top of the salad.

For the dressing, combine salad oil, vinegar, chilli powder, salt, and freshly ground pepper. Sprinkle over salad just before serving. Makes 8 servings.

20. Antipasto Salad

Anyone who has eaten in Italian restaurants is familiar with *antipasto*, the traditional Italian appetizers. These are tempting morsels of such foods as anchovies, cheese, pickled vegetables, salami, and tuna fish. Why not combine some of these piquantly flavoured foods with salad greens to serve as a first course at lunch or dinner? I have tried various combinations for 'antipasto salads' with great success.

The basic plan of an antipasto salad is simple. You just arrange a bed of salad greens in your salad bowl, then top the greens with a colourful array of any of the foods you might find on a tray of antipasto. Bring it to the table to show off the colourful arrangement, then mix with a simple oil and wine vinegar dressing. The result: a robust first course for a summer dinner, or a main dish to serve with hot crisp rolls for lunch or a light supper.

For the salad greens, choose escarole, cos, or leaf lettuce, or heart of lettuce. Add a bit of chicory or dandelion greens, if available, for the sharp, bitter tang they contribute. Tear the salad greens into bite-size pieces as you would for a regular green salad, or shred them. Either way, make a bed of crisp greens in a well-chilled salad bowl.

Now let your imagination, your sense of colour and flavour, and the contents of your kitchen cupboard dictate the assortment you choose for the antipasto toppings: tinned tuna fish, drained and flaked; anchovy fillets, rolled or plain; green or ripe olives, chopped or sliced; hard-boiled eggs, chopped or sliced; salami, shredded or cut in pieces; radish slices; green pepper, chopped or sliced; minced parsley; pimiento strips; chopped spring onions; pickled artichoke hearts, halved or quartered; pickled mushrooms, sliced; Italian pickled vegetables, drained and chopped; fresh tomatoes, chopped or cut in wedges. When you've made your choice, arrange the foods attractively on the salad greens.

DRESSING:
To blend the hearty flavours of an antipasto salad, a very plain oil and vinegar dressing is best. I suggest 1 part red wine vinegar with 3 parts mildly flavoured olive oil, or 2 parts olive oil and 1 part arachide oil. Use garlic-flavoured vinegar or oil if you wish, or rub the salad bowl with a cut clove of garlic before you add the salad greens. Add dressing and toss salad just before serving.

21. Greek Salad

1 lettuce
1 small cos lettuce
18 medium-sized radishes
¼ lb. crumbled cheese
1 small tin (2 oz.) anchovy fillets, minced
2 medium-sized tomatoes, cut in small pieces
1 tablespoon chopped fresh parsley
¼ teaspoon crushed or dried oregano
Freshly ground black pepper

DRESSING:
¼ pint olive oil
2 tablespoons tarragon vinegar
½ teaspoon salt
¼ teaspoon freshly ground pepper
1½ tablespoons mixed fresh herbs (marjoram, rosemary, tarragon, savory, chives, chervil, or parsley)
2 bunches spring onions and tops, neatly trimmed

Two hours before serving, tear the lettuces into a salad bowl. Add whole radishes, cheese, anchovy fillets, tomatoes, parsley, oregano, and pepper. Toss gently. Cover with a damp tea towel, and chill.

For the dressing shake oil, vinegar, salt, pepper, and herbs together in a pint bottle. When ready to serve, pour dressing over salad and toss. Poke spring onions straight up in centre of salad. Makes 6 to 8 servings.

22. Green Goddess Salad

8 to 10 anchovy fillets
1 spring onion
2 tablespoons minced parsley
2 tablespoons minced fresh
  tarragon or 1 tablespoon dried
  tarragon soaked in vinegar
  and then strained
2 tablespoons finely chopped
  chives
1½ pints mayonnaise
½ gill tarragon vinegar
1 peeled clove garlic
1 large cos lettuce
1 lb. cooked lobster, shrimp,
  crab meat, or chicken

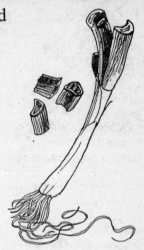

This famous salad was first created in 1915 at the Palace Hotel in honour of George Arliss, who was then appearing in San Francisco in William Archer's play *The Green Goddess*. There are many variations to this creamy dressing. Some cooks use soured cream for part of the mayonnaise and anchovy paste instead of the fillets. Others use a blender to chop together the parsley, tarragon, chives, and anchovy fillets. A well-seasoned French dressing may be used instead of the vinegar.

Chop the anchovies and spring onion together until finely minced. Add parsley, tarragon, and chives, and mix lightly. Turn into a bowl and stir in mayonnaise and vinegar, mixing well. Rub a salad bowl with 1 cut clove of garlic and tear lettuce into bite-size pieces into the bowl.
  Pour over enough dressing to moisten (about 1 pint). Toss lightly. Spoon on salad plates, and garnish with desired shellfish or chicken. Makes 6 servings. Recipe makes about 1 quart dressing, or enough for 12 servings. (You can store the leftover dressing in a covered container in the refrigerator for at least a week.)

Fruit Salads

Fruit Salads

A fruit salad is a refreshing finish to many meals. For sheer beauty, there is no better choice. Combining fresh fruits in a salad is one of the best ways to show off their beautiful colours and shapes, and when fresh fruit is not in season, tinned and frozen can be substituted to compose a lovely salad.

If you wish to introduce fruit to a buffet table, why not arrange a 'fruit salad bar'? Serve platters of assorted fruits, attractively arranged in rows, such as: slices of dessert apples, peeled bananas, and pears, and wedges of avocados, all dipped in lemon or grapefruit juice, stemmed black and green grapes, sliced peeled seedless oranges, small pineapple rings. Offer with the fruit a choice of cream or whipped cream and a dressing. Some prefer a dressing made of soured cream, others a thin mayonnaise, made with lemon juice. The accompaniment is a matter of choice.

When arranging the buffet, place chilled salad plates nearby, and if you like the Transcontinental way of serving fruit with crisp salad greens, stand a bowl at the side, and let guests make their own salads and choose their own dressing.

When grapefruit or other juicy fruit is to be mixed with the salad greens, it is a good idea to toss the lettuce with the dressing first and then arrange the fruit over the salad, so that the fruit retains its shape and the juices do not dilute the dressing.

23. Fresh Fruit Salad with Cranberry Dressing

4 tablespoons mayonnaise
¼ pint jellied cranberry sauce
Juice of ½ lemon
Juice of ½ small orange
¼ teaspoon dry mustard
2 teaspoons caster sugar
1 large fresh pineapple or 1 tin
   (1 lb. 4 oz.) sliced pineapple
Crisp lettuce or other greens
3 bananas
2 or 3 soft ripe peaches

Fresh fruits of the autumn season make a colourful salad plate, especially when you serve a bowl of this unusual cranberry dressing to top each salad. You might scatter pomegranate seeds over each salad for extra brightness.

For the dressing blend together mayonnaise, cranberry sauce, lemon juice, orange juice, mustard, and sugar. Chill. Peel pineapple and slice, removing core. On to 6 to 8 individual salad plates covered with crisp salad greens, arrange a slice of pineapple. Peel and slice bananas into the centre of the pineapple ring, and arrange sliced peaches in spoke fashion on top. Pass the dressing separately for each diner to serve himself. Makes 6 to 8 servings.

24. Waldorf Salad

6 firm, tart, red apples
2 tablespoons lemon juice
1½ cups sliced celery
3 oz. coarsely chopped walnuts
Salad dressing or mayonnaise
   (about 1½ gills)
1 medium sized lettuce

Wash apples. Quarter, core, and dice coarsely without peeling. Sprinkle with lemon juice and toss to prevent discoloration. Add celery, nuts, and salad dressing or mayonnaise to moisten well. Serve at once on crisp lettuce. Makes 6 servings.

25. Fruit Salad in Cos Lettuce Leaves

1 lb. cottage cheese
¼ teaspoon seasoned salt
3 tablespoons mayonnaise
*2 oz. coarsely chopped pecans,
    cashews, or walnuts*
*⅔ pint cut-up fruit or whole
    berries (such as cantaloup or
    honeydew melon, fresh peaches,
    grapes, strawberries)*
*6 medium-sized cos lettuce
    leaves*

MINT DRESSING:
¼ pint mint jelly
½ gill salad oil
¼ teaspoon grated lime peel
2 or 3 tablespoons lime juice
Salt

Combine cottage cheese, seasoned salt, and mayonnaise. Gently stir in nuts and fruit. Spoon some of the fruit and cheese mixture into each lettuce leaf. Arrange filled leaves on a large platter. Serve with Mint Dressing. Makes 6 servings.

Beat mint jelly with a rotary beater until smooth. Add salad oil, lime peel, lime juice, and a few grains of salt. Stir until blended. Makes about 1½ gills dressing.

26. California Fruit Salad

Arrange, alternately, sections of peeled fresh grapefruit, avocado slices, and peeled orange sections on a bed of chicory, and sprinkle rather thickly with minced green and red bell peppers. Serve with French dressing.

27. Fruit Salad with Pecan Dressing

¼ pint salad oil
½ gill orange juice
1 tablespoon lemon juice
1 teaspoon caster sugar
¼ teaspoon salt
½ gill finely chopped, toasted
    pecans
1 cup cubed fresh or tinned
    pineapple
3 bananas, sliced
½ lb. seedless or seeded grapes
2 pears, peeled and diced
2 red-skinned apples, diced

This tart salad dressing includes chopped nuts. If pecans are not available substitute cashew nuts. Melon cubes would make a good addition to the fresh fruit combination.

Pour salad oil and orange juice into a 1-pint screw-top jar or plastic shaker. Add lemon juice, sugar, salt, and chopped nuts. (If you toast pecans in a moderate oven (350°F) for 10 minutes, they are more crisp and flavourful.) Cover tightly and shake until dressing is mixed thoroughly. Makes ½ pint dressing. Toss together chilled pineapple, sliced bananas, grapes, diced pears, and diced apples. Pour dressing over fruit and toss lightly. Makes 7 or 8 servings.

28. Apple and Cauliflower Salad

1½–2 lb. thinly sliced unpeeled
    dessert apples
6 oz. thinly sliced raw
    cauliflower
Mayonnaise (about 1½ gills)
Salt and pepper
5–6 lettuce cups

Cut apple slices in thirds, crosswise. Toss with cauliflower and enough mayonnaise to coat each piece. Season to taste with salt and pepper. (Add a little lemon juice if you like a more tart salad.) Chill thoroughly and serve in lettuce cups. Makes 5 to 6 servings.

29. Mexican Salad

8 small cooked beetroot
4 peeled oranges
4 unpeeled, cored red apples
4 peeled bananas
Fruit from 1 fresh pineapple, or
    1 tin (1lb. 4 oz.) pineapple
    chunks
3 limes, peeled
1 medium-sized lettuce
2 oz. caster sugar (optional)
Seeds of 2 ripe pomegranates
6 oz. peanuts, chopped
½ pint tart French dressing
    (1½ gills oil, ¼ cup red wine
    vinegar, salt) or ½ pint
    orange juice

Slice or dice the beetroot and various fruits and shred the lettuce. Put lettuce in the bottom of a large shallow bowl and arrange fruits and all other ingredients in layers, sprinkling with the sugar, if you choose to use it. Have the top layer pictorially attractive, perhaps with a ring of oranges around the outer edge, then beetroot, then pineapple in the centre, with pomegranate seeds and chopped peanuts sprinkled over all. Just before serving, pour on the French dressing, or the orange juice (which the Mexicans sometimes prefer), and mix gently. Makes about 8 servings.

30. Bacon and Apple Salad

8 oz. crumbled fried bacon
¼ pint diced apple
¼ pint sliced celery
4 tablespoons mayonnaise
4 lettuce cups

Combine crumbled bacon, apple, celery, and mayonnaise. You may wish to add some lemon or orange juice if the apples are not very tart and juicy. Serve in lettuce cups. Makes 4 servings.

T – P.S.B. – B

31. Creamy Waldorf Salad

3 oz. cream cheese
½ gill evaporated milk
2 teaspoons caster sugar
¾ teaspoon salt
Dash of pepper
1 tablespoon vinegar
¾–1 lb. diced, unpared apples
5–6 oz. diced celery
1½ oz. finely chopped nuts
  (optional)

A piquant cream cheese dressing is prepared in advance and chilled for this interesting variation of the classic Waldorf salad. Apples, celery, and nuts are added just before serving.

Put cream cheese into a bowl. Gradually stir in evaporated milk, mixing until smooth. Add sugar, salt, pepper, and vinegar; beat until smooth and fluffy. Chill. Just before time to serve, add apples, celery, and nuts. Toss lightly with a fork. Serve on lettuce. Makes 4 servings.

32. Autumn Fruit and Nut Tray

From fruits in season – such as apples, pears, figs, pineapple, peaches, bananas, grapes, and cooked quinces – select an assortment of your favourites. Allow 1 or 2 whole fruits, or about 1 cup fruit for each serving. Prepare fruit to eat: peel, seed, and core as is necessary. Cut fruit in about two-bite-size portions (but cut grapes in halves) and arrange each fruit individually in a row on a large tray. Garnish with salted nuts if you wish or serve the nuts in a separate bowl. Let each person select the combination for his own salad. Spoon dressing over each serving, or serve with cream if preferred.

CHEESE AND NUT DRESSING:
Whip until smooth 8 oz. cream cheese with ½ gill milk and 1½ tablespoons lemon juice. Blend ¼ pint finely chopped salted cashew nuts with 4 oz. grated sharp Cheddar cheese, ½ tablespoon caster sugar, ¼ teaspoon pepper, and salt to taste. Add more milk if you prefer a thinner dressing. Makes about 1½ pints.

33. Cheese and Apple Salad

¼ pint chopped red-skinned apple
¼ pint sliced celery
2 oz. Cheddar cheese, cut in
 ½-inch cubes
¼ pint diced pineapple, fresh or
 tinned
4 tablespoons mayonnaise
3 tablespoons lemon juice
1 teaspoon caster sugar
¼ teaspoon salt
5–6 lettuce cups

Combine the apple, celery, cheese, and pineapple. Stir the mayonnaise, lemon juice, sugar, and salt together until smooth. Pour over apple mixture and stir until well coated. Chill. To serve, spoon into crisp lettuce cups. Makes 5 to 6 servings.

34. Avocado Halves with Citrus Dressing

2 oz. icing sugar
¼ tablespoon paprika
1¼ teaspoons salt
1 clove garlic, peeled and cut in half
¾ tablespoon Worcester sauce
½ pint salad oil
3 tablespoons lemon juice
3 tablespoons tarragon vinegar
¼ pint orange juice
4 medium-sized avocados
Curly endive as required

Because it contains a large amount of acid, this orange-coloured dressing keeps the avocado from darkening.

Put the sugar, paprika, salt, garlic, and Worcester sauce in a quart jar. Pour in the oil, lemon juice, vinegar, and orange juice. Cover and shake until well blended. Let stand several hours for flavours to blend. Remove garlic and shake again before using. Cut avocados in half lengthwise, remove stones (do not peel), and arrange on endive. Spoon dressing into cavities and over fruit. Makes 8 servings (dressing makes about 1 pint).

35. Avocado-Popcorn Salad

For a real conversation piece, place half of an unpeeled avocado on a bed of lettuce. Then fill the cavity with hot buttered popped corn. Sprinkle with rum or lemon juice. Serve at once.

36. Grapes in Avocado Half Shells

3 medium-sized avocados
1 tablespoon lemon juice
Salt
1 lb. red grapes
¼ cup sliced celery (use white
    inner stalks)
¼ gill lime juice
¼ gill unsweetened pineapple
    juice
¼ pint red table wine
1¼ teaspoons caster sugar
¼ teaspoon brine from pickled
    hot peppers
Endive or chicory
Mint

This fruit platter, with its striking colour combination of ruby, white, and avocado green, is ideal for a buffet.

Cut avocados in half lengthwise and remove stones; brush with lemon juice and sprinkle lightly with salt. Cut grapes in half, remove seeds, and combine with the sliced celery. Spoon mixture into the avocado centres.

Mix together lime juice, pineapple juice, wine, sugar, and pepper brine. Pour over the stuffed avocados. Chill. Serve on a bed of endive or chicory, and garnish with mint. Makes 6 servings.

37. Avocado, Pear, and Pineapple Salad

Peel 4 avocados and peel and core 4 pears (choose ones of about equal size). Slice, dice, or cut fruit in crescents. Arrange in a ring or pinwheel fashion on a bed of cos and Webbs Wonder lettuce with ½ pint finely chopped fresh, frozen, or tinned pineapple in the centre. Sprinkle with lemon juice. Pour a plain French dressing over salad and serve. Makes 8 to 10 servings.

38. Curried Avocado Rings

1 large avocado
Lemon juice
3 oz. cream cheese
2 tablespoons crumbled blue cheese
3 tablespoons each chopped ripe olives and nuts
1 tablespoon chopped chives
Grated peel and juice of 1 lime
2 teaspoons evaporated milk or light cream
¾ teaspoon curry powder
¼ teaspoon salt
Dash of cayenne
Crisp salad greens
Grapefruit sections
French dressing

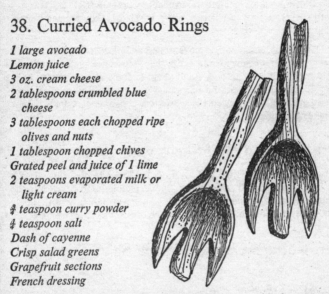

Because these avocado rings are so attractive, they are ideal to serve at a luncheon party. The rich curry-seasoned filling is especially appealing.

Cut avocado in half, remove stone, and peel. Enlarge the cavity in each half by scooping out some of the avocado. (This may be mashed and combined with cream cheese for a sandwich filling.) Brush avocado halves with lemon juice. Combine cream cheese, blue cheese, olives, nuts, chives, grated lime peel and juice, milk, curry powder, salt, and cayenne. Pack cheese mixture into avocado halves, press halves together; wrap in foil and chill. To serve, cut stuffed avocado crosswise into 6 slices Place each round on crisp salad greens. Garnish with grapefruit sections, and serve with a tart French dressing. Makes 6 servings.

39. Baked Avocado Halves

2 firm, medium-sized avocados
1 egg white
4 tablespoons mayonnaise
Pinch of salt
4 lettuce cups

The dressing bakes right into this avocado to offset the richness. Garnish with slivers of cooked chicken breast if salad is required for a main course.

Peel avocados, cut in half, remove stones, and place in a lightly greased baking tin. Beat egg white until stiff, then fold in mayonnaise and salt. Pile mixture lightly into avocado cavities. Bake in a moderate oven (350°F.) for 8 minutes. Slip pan under grill for several minutes, until meringue is lightly browned. Place in lettuce cups and serve immediately. Makes 4 servings.

40. Avocado Half Shells with Caviar

For each serving arrange half an unpeeled avocado on a bed of crisp lettuce on individual salad plates. Spoon 1 tablespoon caviar into the centre of each avocado half shell, and garnish lightly with finely chopped white onion. Pour plain French dressing over filling.

41. Cottage Cheese–Banana Salad

4 or 5 ripe bananas
1 cos and 1 cabbage lettuce
Barely 1 lb. cottage cheese
½ pint whole cranberry sauce
Chopped salted almonds
  (optional)

Cranberry sauce makes a sweet-tart dressing for this cottage cheese salad. Tinned or fresh pear halves can be used in place of the bananas.

Peel bananas, cut in half lengthwise, then arrange on lettuce leaves. Spread a layer of cottage cheese over the top of each banana half, then top with a spoonful of cranberry sauce. Sprinkle with chopped nuts if desired. Makes 8 to 10 servings.

42. Avocado Halves with Hot Cocktail Sauce

2 oz. butter or margarine
¼ gill tomato ketchup
2 tablespoons vinegar
2 tablespoons water
½ tablespoon caster sugar
2 teaspoons Worcester sauce
¼ teaspoon salt
Dash of Tabasco
3 small avocados

For an easy-to-make appetizer, fill avocado half shells with this heated, spicy sauce which will contrast with the cool, butter-smooth avocado.

In the top of a double boiler, mix the butter with the ketchup, vinegar, water, sugar, Worcester sauce, salt, and Tabasco to taste. Stir over boiling water until butter has melted, the sugar has dissolved, and sauce is smooth. Cut avocados in half lengthwise, separate halves, and remove stones. Spoon hot sauce into avocados and serve as an appetizer. Makes 6 servings.

43. Grapefruit–Avocado Salad

1 large grapefruit
2 medium-sized avocados
1 curly endive
1 pimiento
½ pint tart French dressing

The feathery curls of endive make an ideal background for grapefruit and avocado. With its sharp contrasts in flavour and texture, this salad makes an excellent accompaniment to cold duck, goose, or pork.

Cut grapefruit into segments and remove membrane. Peel avocado and cut in slices about ¾ inch wide, or the width of the grapefruit segments. Tear endive into small pieces and arrange on 4 salad plates, with the lighter coloured leaves in the centre. On each bed of endive, alternate 4 avocado slices and 3 grapefruit sections, arranging them to form a compact half circle. Cut pimiento along one of its folded sides into four 1-inch strips about ⅛ inch wide, and arrange in a V over the pointed end of the avocado slices. Shake the French dressing well and pour over. Makes 4 servings.

44. Avocado Half Shells with Mandarin Oranges

Cut 1 medium-sized avocado in half. Remove stones, and sprinkle cut sides with lemon juice. Arrange on salad plates on a bed of endive. Spoon tinned mandarin orange sections into each avocado cavity and pour French dressing over avocado and endive. Makes 2 servings.

45. Curried Banana Salad

3 medium-sized bananas
1 tablespoon lemon juice
6–8 oz. cooked rice, chilled
2 tablespoons sliced celery
3 oz. seedless grapes
2 oz. finely chopped salted peanuts
1 tablespoon minced chives
2 tablespoons tinned
  pimientos, cut in fine strips
Few drops Tabasco

DRESSING :
¼ pint mayonnaise
2 tablespoons light cream
1 tablespoon lemon juice or
  lime juice
1 teaspoon curry powder
¼ teaspoon dry mustard
Chicory or other crisp greens
1 tablespoon toasted coconut
2 tablespoons chopped chutney

You can make this curry-flavoured fruit salad before it is needed. It's a fine accompaniment to cold chicken, lamb, fish, or shellfish.

Cut the bananas in ½-inch slices. Sprinkle immediately with the lemon juice. Add rice, celery, grapes, peanuts, chives, pimiento, and Tabasco. Toss lightly. Chill.

Combine the mayonnaise with cream, lemon juice, curry, and mustard. To serve, add dressing to the salad. Toss lightly with 2 forks. Arrange on chilled salad greens. Sprinkle with coconut and top with a small mound of chutney. Makes 4 to 6 servings.

46. Citrus Lettuce Salad

1 large lettuce
½ bunch watercress
1 grapefruit, sectioned
2 medium-sized oranges,
*   sectioned*
12 dates, stoned
2 oz. chopped preserved ginger
3 oz. cream cheese

Some unusual ingredients, including orange and grapefruit sections, dates, and watercress, make this lettuce salad quite a surprise.

Tear lettuce and watercress into bite-size pieces in a salad bowl. Add grapefruit and orange sections, dates, ginger, and just enough Citrus Dressing to moisten slightly. Crumble cream cheese into salad and toss lightly. Makes about 5 servings.

CITRUS DRESSING:
Combine in a covered jar 4 oz. caster sugar, 4 tablespoons each vinegar and tomato ketchup, 1 teaspoon salt, 1 small finely chopped onion, and 1 clove garlic, minced or mashed. Add enough salad oil (about ½ pint) to make nearly a pint of dressing. Cover, shake well, and chill.

47. Fruit and Vegetable Salad

1 large tin (1 lb. 14 oz.) fruit
*   cocktail*
1 medium tin (11 oz.) mandarin
*   orange sections*
¾ lb. raw shredded carrots
1 medium-sized lettuce, finely
*   chopped*
Pinch of salt
Mayonnaise and lemon juice
*   to taste*

Drain the juice from the fruit cocktail and the mandarin oranges. Combine fruit with the carrots and the lettuce. Toss with salt and enough mayonnaise to moisten. Taste, then add lemon juice to give mixture sufficient tartness. Makes 6 or 7 servings.

48. Cherry Fruit Salad

1 iceberg lettuce
1 medium-sized cantaloup,
peeled and cut in cubes
1 small pineapple, peeled and
cut in chunks or 1 tin (1 lb. 13
oz.) pineapple chunks,
drained
1 avocado, peeled and diced
¾ lb. stoned cherries
½ teaspoon salt
Juice of ½ lemon

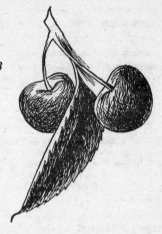

DRESSING:
2 tablespoons sesame seeds
½ pint soured cream
Juice of 1 lime
3 tablespoons orange juice
¼ teaspoon salt

Line a salad bowl with lettuce cups and tear the remaining lettuce into bite-size chunks. Lightly toss the lettuce chunks with the cantaloup, pineapple, avocado, cherries, salt, and lemon juice. Pile in the salad bowl. Chill.

For the dressing, sprinkle the sesame seeds in a shallow baking tin and toast in a moderate oven (350°F.) for 10 minutes, or until golden brown. Mix the soured cream with the lime juice, orange juice, salt, and toasted sesame seeds. Serve in a separate dish to accompany the salad. Makes 6 servings.

NOTE: If sesame seeds are not available, substitute chopped cashew nuts.

49. Minted Citrus Salad

On a bed of salad greens (leaf lettuce or cos lettuce tips) arrange 2 cups fresh grapefruit sections and 2 or 3 large seedless oranges, peeled and thinly sliced. Garnish with mint leaves. Ladle some of this dressing on each serving: Blend 3 tablespoons mint jelly with 1 tablespoon honey, grated peel and juice of 1 lime, and juice of 1 lemon. Makes 6 servings.

50. Orange Salad

1 medium-sized lettuce
2 medium-sized tomatoes,
  peeled and thinly sliced
Salt and freshly ground pepper
1 small onion, very thinly sliced
  crosswise
1 or 2 teaspoons vinegar
2 large oranges, peeled (remove
  white membrane) and sliced
  crosswise
1 teaspoon caster sugar
Tinned or cooked beetroot
  slices cut in star shapes
Radish 'roses' or 'tulips'

The intriguing blend of orange, onion, and tomatoes with vinegar and sugar, and no other dressing, makes this salad an especially good choice for those who are counting calories. It also makes an ideal accompaniment to cold duck, goose, or pork.

Arrange outer leaves of lettuce in bottom of a salad bowl. Save the heart to use as garnish. Lay tomato slices on lettuce. Season with salt and pepper. Distribute onion slices over tomatoes. Salt, pepper, and sprinkle with vinegar. Arrange orange slices on onions, and sprinkle with sugar. Refrigerate for 15 minutes. Garnish with lettuce heart, cut in 6 portions, beetroot stars, and radish flowers. Makes 6 servings.

51. Orange and Beetroot Salad Plate

Citrus fruits give the sharp tang sometimes required in a salad. Try this teaming of fresh orange slices and sliced beetroot for a colourful citrus salad.

Alternate slices of orange and beetroot on a bed of curly endive or watercress and serve with this dressing: Mix 6 tablespoons salad oil with 2 tablespoons vinegar, ¼ teaspoon prepared mustard, 1 teaspoon finely chopped parsley, and ½ teaspoon each dried chervil and tarragon. Makes ¼ pint dressing.

52. Crunchy Fruit Salad

1 tin (3 oz.) crisp Chinese
noodles
3 medium-sized oranges
1½ gills tinned or fresh grape-
fruit segments
¼ pint pineapple chunks
¼ gill French dressing
Toasted sesame seeds

Crisp Chinese noodles replace lettuce in this fruit salad. It is an especially good accompaniment to roast pork or spare ribs. To toast sesame seeds, place in a heavy frying pan. Stir over medium heat until browned, in about 5 minutes.

Arrange beds of noodles on 5 individual salad plates. Peel oranges and cut in ¼-inch-thick slices. Arrange sliced oranges, well-drained grapefruit segments, and pineapple chunks on noodles. Just before serving, pour French dressing over each salad, then sprinkle to taste with toasted sesame seeds, or split fried almonds. Makes 5 servings.

53. Orange, Onion, and Olive Salad

3 medium-sized oranges
1 mild onion
1 dozen stoned ripe olives, sliced
¼ lb. Roquefort cheese
1 clove garlic, minced or mashed
¼ pint French dressing
6 lettuce cups

The Roquefort cheese dressing gives this orange and onion salad a new accent. Grapefruit segments from which all the white membrane has been removed may be added just before serving.

Peel oranges and cut in slices crosswise. Peel onion and cut in very thin slices. Toss onion and oranges together in a bowl with the sliced ripe olives. Mash the Roquefort cheese in a bowl, stir in the garlic, then moisten with the French dressing. Pour over the oranges and onion and let marinate for 1 hour. Serve in crisp lettuce cups. Makes 6 servings.

54. Citrus Salad

1 tablespoon honey
2 tablespoons tarragon vinegar
1 teaspoon ground cardamom
5 or 6 dashes of Angostura bitters
¼ teaspoon onion salt
2 fresh grapefruit
3 large oranges

You won't notice that oil is missing from the dressing on this salad. All other ingredients combine to cut down the sharpness of the citrus fruits. Tinned, unsweetened grapefruit segments may be used as a substitute for the fresh.

Blend the honey with the vinegar, cardamom, bitters, and onion salt. Cut grapefruit into segments. Slice oranges. Toss together with dressing. Serve as a bowl salad, with or without lettuce. Makes 6 servings.

55. Grapefruit Pinwheels with Cheese-stuffed Prunes

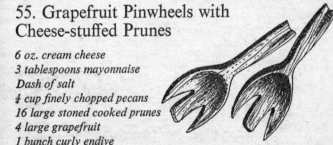

6 oz. cream cheese
3 tablespoons mayonnaise
Dash of salt
¼ cup finely chopped pecans
16 large stoned cooked prunes
4 large grapefruit
1 bunch curly endive

No dressing is needed for this combination of grapefruit sections and spicy sweet prunes, plumped with cheese and pecans.

Cream the cheese (warmed to room temperature), with the mayonnaise, and salt. Stir in the nuts. Stuff some of the cheese mixture into each prune. Peel and section grapefruit. For each serving arrange 6 or 7 fresh grapefruit sections in the shape of a pinwheel on a bed of endive on salad plates. Centre 2 stuffed prunes in each pinwheel. Makes 8 servings.

56. Cranberry Grape Salad

1 lb. cranberries
8–9 oz. caster sugar
¾ lb. grapes, halved and seeded
1 cup sliced celery
4 oz. chopped nuts
12 marshmallows, quartered
½ pint whipping cream
Lettuce as required

You sugar the ground raw cranberries to draw out their scarlet juice, which literally dyes this salad a rosy red. The juicy grapes lend a crackling bite. This fruit combination is sweet enough for dessert.

Put cranberries through your mincer, fitted with a fine blade, into a medium-sized bowl. Add sugar and let stand while you assemble the other ingredients. Stir the grapes, celery, nuts, and marshmallows into the cranberries. Whip cream and fold in thoroughly. Chill for several hours. Serve in lettuce cups. Makes 12 servings.

57. Grape Jumble Salad

Segments from ½ medium-sized
  grapefruit
6 oz. seedless grapes
1 fresh pear, peeled, cored,
  and diced
1 tin (11 oz.) mandarin
  oranges, drained
4 tablespoons olive or salad oil
1 tablespoon each lemon and
  lime juice
1 teaspoon salt
¼ teaspoon paprika
Few grains cayenne
Chicory and watercress

Place grapefruit segments in a bowl with grapes, diced pear, and oranges. Combine olive oil, lemon juice, lime juice, salt, paprika, and cayenne. Pour over fruit, and toss together lightly. Chill in refrigerator. Serve on crisp salad greens. Makes 6 servings.

58. Tomato and Cantaloup Ball Salad

1 small cantaloup
2 tomatoes
¼ pint French dressing
Salt and pepper to taste
2 sprigs mint (optional)
Curly endive
  as required
Lime or lemon wedges

Cantaloup half shells serve as the bowls for this simple, good-looking salad.

Cut cantaloup in half, remove seeds, and scoop the pulp into balls. Cut the stem end from the tomatoes and cut in wedges. Mix the cantaloup balls and tomato wedges and refill each half shell. Sprinkle with French dressing, and salt and pepper to taste. Garnish with mint. Serve on a bed of endive. Garnish each salad with a wedge of lime or lemon for added tang. Makes 2 servings.

59. Cantaloup and Cherry Salad

Peel 1 ripe cantaloup. Cut into slices about 1 inch wide, and remove seeds. Put each melon ring on a plate and fill the centre with stoned dark, sweet cherries. Serve with whipped cream. Makes 6 to 8 servings.

NOTE : If preferred, place rings on a bed of lettuce and serve with French dressing.

60. Cantaloup and Onion Salad

1½ pints cantaloup balls
2 small onions
1 medium-sized lettuce
1½ gills tart French dressing

Pair cantaloup balls with onions that are mild and sweet in flavour.

Chill cantaloup balls. Cut onions in half and thinly slice. Shred lettuce. Mix chilled melon balls with onions and lettuce. Toss with French dressing to taste. Makes 10 servings.

61. Fruit Salad Plate

Toss together a mixture of cantaloup cubes, slightly crushed and sweetened raspberries, and banana slices. Heap on a plate lined with salad greens and garnish with lemon or lime wedges. Allow about ½ pint for each serving.

62. Tropical Salad

1 small papaya or ripe melon
2 slices (1 inch thick) fresh
pineapple
¼ pint tinned or frozen pineapple
pieces
1 tin (14 oz.) mangoes
2 medium-sized oranges

AVOCADO DRESSING:
1 large ripe avocado
¼ pint orange juice
1½ teaspoons lemon juice
1½ teaspoons caster sugar
¼ teaspoon salt
Watercress as required

Here's a recipe for a salad which calls for fruits of both subtropical and tropical origin. The avocado dressing, with its bright green colour, is the ideal foil for the yellow and orange-coloured fruits.

Cut papaya or melon in half, scrape out seeds, peel, and dice. Cut fresh pineapple slices, if used, in pieces. Cut mangoes into small pieces or slices. Peel oranges, removing all membrane. Slice, then cut into pieces. Combine all fruits and chill.

Cut avocado in half, remove the stone, peel, and mash. Add orange juice, lemon juice, sugar, and salt gradually. Beat thoroughly. Chill.

Arrange chilled fruits on bed of watercress and serve with the avocado dressing. Makes 6 to 8 servings.

63. Melon and Grape Salad

Prepare 1½ pints of cubes, slices, or slim crescents of peeled and seeded melon, such as cantaloup, Charentais, or honeydew. Choose your favourite or use a combination of several varieties. Arrange on a tray with 12 oz. of seedless or seeded grapes. Serve dressing separately.

Use the first dressing if you like your dressing light and tart, the second if you prefer it rich and creamy, or perhaps you would like to offer both. Makes 5 or 6 servings.

LIGHT TART DRESSING:
Shake 1 teaspoon grated lemon or lime peel with 4 tablespoons lemon or lime juice, ½ tablespoon honey, and ¼ teaspoon salt.

CREAMY DRESSING:
Blend 1½ gills soured cream with 3 tablespoons lemon or lime juice, ½ teaspoon each grated lemon and orange peel, ½ teaspoon minced preserved ginger, and 1 tablespoon caster sugar.

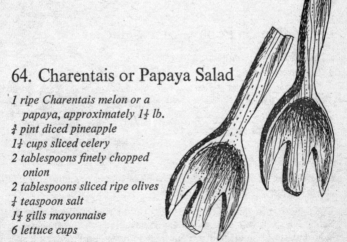

64. Charentais or Papaya Salad

1 ripe Charentais melon or a
  papaya, approximately 1½ lb.
¾ pint diced pineapple
1¼ cups sliced celery
2 tablespoons finely chopped
  onion
2 tablespoons sliced ripe olives
¼ teaspoon salt
1½ gills mayonnaise
6 lettuce cups

Cut the melon or papaya in half lengthwise and remove seeds. Remove pulp, dice it, and place in a mixing bowl. Combine with pineapple, celery, onion, olives, salt, and mayonnaise. Chill. Serve in lettuce cups. Makes 6 servings.

65. Melon, Orange, Avocado Salad

Peel 1 ripe melon (1–1½ lb.). Cut in halves or quarters and remove seeds. Peel 3 medium-sized oranges, cutting away white membrane. Slice thinly crosswise, removing as many seeds as possible. Peel, cut in halves, and stone 2 ripe avocados. Let fruit marinade several hours in chilli dressing in refrigerator. Drain and arrange on tray. Offer dressing with each serving. Makes 4 servings.

CHILLI DRESSING:
Combine ½ gill each salad oil and lemon juice, 1 tablespoon finely minced spring onion, ½ teaspoon chilli powder, ½ teaspoon salt, and ¼ teaspoon freshly ground black pepper.

66. Melon or Papaya Star Salad

2 ripe melons or papayas
¼ lb. cottage cheese,
  pineapple-flavoured if possible
3 oz. cream cheese
¼ teaspoon salt
2 tablespoons lemon juice
Lettuce
French dressing as required

Cheese complements the delicate flavour of melon or papaya in this salad. It is attractive in appearance, too.

Cut tops from melons or papayas about a quarter of the way down. Scoop out seeds with a teaspoon. Combine cottage and cream cheeses, salt, and lemon juice, and mix until smooth. Spoon into fruit cases, packing down as much as possible. Chill 1 to 2 hours. Cut crosswise in 1½-inch slices, and serve on lettuce or leaf-garnished salad plates with a simple French dressing or a sprinkling of lemon juice. Makes 4 to 6 servings.

67. Fruit-filled Water Melon Shell with Tart Sauce

1 large, ripe water melon
Selection of fresh fruits
(combine any or all of the
following with bite-size pieces
or balls cut from the water
melon heart: for a large melon
shell, you will need 3 to 4
quarts bite-size fruits and
about 1 quart melon pieces):
Stoned sweet cherries
Ripe melon (other than water
melon), cut into balls or
bite-size pieces
Strawberries
Raspberries
Fresh or tinned pineapple, cut
into chunks
Peaches, sliced
Pears, sliced or diced
Seeded grapes

TART SAUCE
1½ gills fresh orange juice
½ gill fresh lemon juice
2 oz. caster sugar
Dash salt
4 egg yolks, slightly beaten
¾ pint thick cream, whipped
Grated orange peel

Take time to select the right water melon to make the 'boat' for this lavish, fresh fruit salad. It should be a large, ripe, oval-shaped melon that rests securely on one side.

Place washed melon on flat side and cut a large window in the top, removing about ⅓ of the shell. Take out melon heart, leaving a layer of pink to form a bed for the salad. Cut the heart of the melon into balls or bite-size pieces for the fruit salad mixture. Cut a sawtooth edge on melon shell with a sharp knife. Turn upside down and allow to drain thoroughly. Chill. At serving time, fill shell with combined fresh fruit. Serve with Tart Sauce. Makes 15 to 18 servings.

Combine orange and lemon juice, sugar, and salt in top of double boiler. Cook over direct heat, stirring constantly until the sugar has dissolved, and syrup simmers. Place over hot water and gradually add egg yolks, beating constantly. Continue to cook and stir over hot (not boiling) water until smooth and thick. Chill. Fold in whipped cream. Turn into serving bowl. Sprinkle with orange peel.

68. Peach–Cheese Salad

¾ lb. cottage cheese
½ gill mayonnaise
1 cup diced peaches
1 oz. slivered salted almonds
Few grains salt
Shredded lettuce
Sliced peaches
French dressing

You'll find this salad light but filling enough for mid-day meals. The crisp saltiness of the almonds adds interest.

Gently combine all ingredients. Pile attractively on shredded lettuce. Garnish with sliced peaches and serve with a creamy French dressing. Makes 4 servings.

69. Pear–Mango Salad

1 small fresh pineapple
¼ lb. creamed cottage cheese
2 pears, peeled and cut in
   chunks
1 mango, peeled and sliced
1½ tablespoons sliced
   preserved ginger
1½ tablespoons toasted, sliced
   Brazil nuts
Sweet French dressing

Heaped in the pineapple half shells, this attractive fresh fruit and cottage cheese salad tastes as good as it looks.

Beginning at the crown, cut pineapple in half lengthwise. Scoop out the fruit, using a grapefruit knife. In the bottom of each half, place a layer of cottage cheese. Remove core from pineapple and cut fruit into chunks. Place a layer over the cottage cheese. Arrange a layer each of pears and mangoes over the pineapple. Top with a sprinkling of ginger and nuts, and serve with a sweet French dressing. Makes 2 servings as a luncheon entrée, or 4 to 6 as an accompaniment.

NOTE: If fresh mango is not available, substitute tinned, cut in slices.

70. Cheese-stuffed Pear Salad

*¼ gill port or other red dessert
  wine*
1 teaspoon cornflour
¼ gill currant jelly
¼ pint mayonnaise
2 teaspoons lemon juice
2 teaspoons grated lemon peel
¼ teaspoon salt
¼ pint whipping cream
Red food colouring
*1 large tin (1 lb. 13 oz.) pear
  halves*
*2 tablespoons crumbled blue
  or Roquefort cheese*
*2 tablespoons grated Cheddar
  cheese*
Salad greens

The currant jelly and wine dressing pick up the mild flavour of pears.
Fresh winter pear halves, brushed with lemon juice, can substitute for
tinned pears.

To make dressing, place wine and cornflour in a saucepan and stir until
blended. Add currant jelly. Stirring constantly, cook until mixture boils.
Cool. Stir in mayonnaise, lemon juice and peel, and salt. Whip cream
until stiff and fold in. Add enough red food colouring to tint dressing a
pale rose colour. Chill.
   Drain pear halves. Blend blue and Cheddar cheeses with a fork. Stuff
the cavities of 4 pear halves with cheese mixture, and put another pear
half on top of each. Poke 2 toothpicks into pear halves to hold in place.
Arrange on salad greens and top with dressing. Makes 4 servings.

71. Peach Compote

Combine equal portions of sliced ripe peaches, melon balls, and fresh
pineapple cubes. Sprinkle with fresh lemon or lime juice and serve chilled
from pineapple shells, as a first course salad or a dessert.

72. Pears with Filbert Cheese Balls

3 oz. very finely chopped
  filberts
8 oz. cream cheese
Pinch of salt
3 tablespoons maraschino
  cherry juice
8 winter pears or 2 tins (1 lb.
  13 oz. each) pear halves
1 cos lettuce or other crisp
  salad greens

Cream cheese balls, tinted with maraschino cherry juice and rolled in chopped roasted filberts, adorn a platter of juicy winter pears or tinned pears.

Place chopped nuts in a shallow baking tin and toast in a slow oven (300°F. or lower) until lightly browned, stirring occasionally. Blend the cream cheese with the salt and cherry juice until cheese is softened. Roll cheese into balls about the size of large marbles, then roll in toasted nuts.

Arrange pear halves, cut side up, on crisp salad greens on a large plate. (If using fresh pears, dip peeled and cored halves in lemon, orange, or pineapple juice to prevent discolouring.) Place two or three cheese balls in the hollow of each pear half. Serve with or without French dressing. Makes 8 servings with 2 halves apiece.

73. Peach Fruit Salad

2 large, ripe peaches
1 avocado
16 grapefruit sections
Shredded lettuce
French dressing

This colour combination of orange, green, and light yellow makes a most attractive first-course salad.

Peel peaches and cut into eighths. Peel avocado, cut into eighths, then cut each in half so that avocado pieces will be the same length as peaches and grapefruit sections. Arrange fruit alternately on bed of shredded lettuce. Serve with French dressing. Makes 4 servings.

74. Stuffed Pear Salad

18 gingersnaps, crushed
¼ pint drained crushed pineapple
8 oz. cream cheese
2 tablespoons mayonnaise
4 fresh winter pears or 8
  tinned pear halves
2 oz. caster sugar
3 tablespoons lemon juice
¼ pint orange juice
1 egg
¼ teaspoon salt
¼ pint whipping cream
Lettuce or watercress

You may stuff either fresh winter pears or tinned Bartletts with this gingersnap and cream cheese filling. The lemon dressing will hold up for several days in your refrigerator, but do not add whipped cream until just before serving.

Mix the crushed gingersnaps, pineapple, cheese, and mayonnaise. Stuff halves of fresh or tinned pears with the mixture and chill.

In a double boiler, mix sugar, lemon and orange juice, well-beaten egg, and salt. Cook over hot water until thickened, stirring constantly. When cool, whip cream and fold into mixture. Arrange pears on crisp lettuce leaves or on sprigs of watercress, and coat with the dressing.

75. Peaches with Horseradish Cream Dressing

3 large ripe peaches, chilled
6 lettuce cups
¼ pint whipping cream
1 tablespoon prepared horseradish
¼ teaspoon salt
Paprika

Cut peaches in half lengthwise. Place each half in a lettuce cup on a salad plate. Whip cream stiffly, and fold in horseradish and salt. Spoon a generous dollop into the centre of each peach half. Dust with paprika. Serve with both a spoon and a fork. Makes 6 servings.

76. Pineapple Salad with Tomato and Avocado

2 cups fresh pineapple chunks
1 cup thinly sliced, peeled
   tomatoes (or cherry tomatoes,
   cut in half)
½ pint diced avocado
4 tablespoons wine vinegar
2 tablespoons salad oil
Salt and freshly ground pepper
   to taste
Salad greens

Combine pineapple chunks, tomatoes, and avocado.

For dressing, beat or shake the wine vinegar with the salad oil, salt, and pepper. Pour over salad and toss lightly. Chill for about 30 minutes. Serve on crisp salad greens (or in the pineapple shell basket described in Recipe 78). Makes about 6 servings.

77. Stuffed Fresh Pineapple Salad

1 medium-sized fresh pineapple
½ pint small curd
   cottage cheese (with chives,
   if desired)
1 stalk celery, finely chopped
1 small avocado
Juice of ½ lemon
4 green or red maraschino
   cherries
Salad greens

With a sharp knife, cut the pineapple in quarters lengthwise, leaving its share of the crown on each piece. Use a grapefruit knife to scoop out the fruit, leaving the shell and foliage intact. Cut off the core and dice the pineapple into a bowl. Stir in the cottage cheese and celery. Fill the shells with the salad mixture. Peel avocado and slice thinly. Arrange 3 or 4 slices over each salad and sprinkle with lemon juice. Top with a cherry. Makes 4 servings.

78. Ideas for Cutting and Serving Fresh Pineapple

When you serve fresh pineapple, you can make it a feast for the eyes as well as the palate by cutting it to take advantage of the natural beauty of the fruit.

If cutting a fresh pineapple is new to you, bear in mind that the core of the fruit is quite fibrous and is usually cut away. Also, you must make your cut far enough inside the shell to remove the eyes. The edible portion that remains will be about half of the whole fruit. The diagrams show basic cutting techniques. Have ready a large heavy knife and also a smaller thin-bladed knife. For cutting neatly along curved edges, you'll need a grapefruit knife.

ZIG-ZAG STYLE

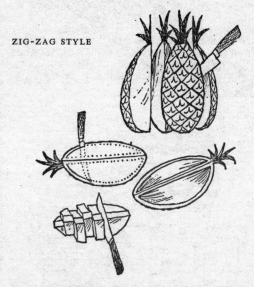

One of the simplest and most impressive ways to present an individual serving of fresh pineapple is what we call zig-zag pineapple. To make 4 servings, cut a medium-sized pineapple as shown in the sketch above. Serve as it is, or set a contrasting fruit in the openings formed by the zig-zag pieces of pineapple. Use any fresh fruit or berries in season: strawberries, papaya pieces, water-melon balls, sweet cherries, or raspberries.

BASKET STYLE

A dramatic way in which to use a large pineapple shell as a serving container for its own fruit is to cut it basket-style. For the simplest version, cut away peel and core from the fruit you remove in cutting the basket, then cut fruit into bite-size chunks and pile back into shell. The pineapple may be combined with other fruits if desired.

FAMILY STYLE

Sometimes you'll prefer simply to prepare the fresh pineapple for eating, without serving it in its shell. The drawings above show the easiest method of removing the peel, saving as much edible fruit as possible (if you wish, you can use the plume as a garnish on a serving tray). Cut the whole fruit into either slices or spears. Slices or spears can be cut in smaller pieces, if desired.

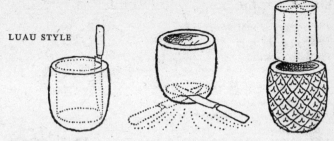

LUAU STYLE

The style of cutting pineapple illustrated above is commonly identified with the Hawaiian feast known as the luau. Pre-cut pineapples with tops set back in place become part of a lavish fruit and flower centre-piece. At a luau the pineapple spears are usually eaten with the fingers.

79. Pineapple Salad with Orange Cottage Cheese

An attractive buffet salad plate can be made with an adaptation of the luau-style of pineapple cutting. Follow first and second steps shown in the sketch above. Then, instead of cutting the whole fruit section into spears, cut crosswise into 4 to 6 thick slices. Cut the hollow pineapple shell crosswise to form a bowl that will hold about 1 pint of Creamy Dressing. Set shell filled with dressing in the centre of a large serving plate or tray. Using a small biscuit cutter, cut out the core of each pineapple slice and arrange slices on lettuce leaves in a circle around the pineapple shell bowl. Top each slice with a scoop of Orange Cottage Cheese. Each guest serves himself a cheese-topped pineapple slice and tops it with dressing. A large pineapple serves 4 to 6. To serve more, you can cut extra slices from a second pineapple.

CREAMY DRESSING:
Whip $\frac{1}{2}$ pint heavy cream with 1 teaspoon dry mustard and $\frac{1}{8}$ teaspoon salt. Fold in $\frac{1}{4}$ pint mayonnaise with 1 tablespoon each of lemon juice and grenadine syrup or maraschino cherry juice, and 2 tablespoons each chopped maraschino cherries and toasted almonds. Makes 1 pint.

ORANGE COTTAGE CHEESE:
Blend 1 pint small curd cottage cheese with 1 teaspoon grated orange peel, and 1 oz. chopped or slivered toasted almonds.

80. Pineapple Salad with Roquefort Dressing

1 oz. crumbled Roquefort cheese
½ pint soured cream
½ gill mayonnaise
Dash of salt
2–3 tablespoons light cream
Fruit from 1 large fresh pine-
apple, cut in quarter slices or
finger shapes
¾ lb. cooked, shelled prawns or
shrimps (if large, cut in
pieces)
Cos lettuce leaves
Paprika to taste

Mash cheese with back of a spoon or fork until soft. Blend with soured cream until smooth. Stir in mayonnaise, salt, and cream. Makes about ¾ pint dressing.

Combine fruit with prawns or shrimps. Toss lightly. Arrange cos lettuce leaves on each salad plate. Top with pineapple mixture. Spoon dressing over, and sprinkle with paprika. Makes 6 to 8 servings.

Vegetable Salads

Vegetable Salads

Vegetable salads may be served all the year round. They are a refreshing addition to any menu, bringing, as they do, crisp freshness to a winter meal and delicious coolness to a summer. You can perk up a family menu or round out a barbecue or picnic meal with a vegetable salad. Some are hearty enough to be main courses at luncheon. Others are elegant enough to sparkle on a party buffet table.

A vegetable salad, of course, can be only as good as the vegetables that go into it. Select high-quality fresh vegetables, and prepare them with care. Many vegetables, such as asparagus, broccoli, cauliflower, mushrooms, zucchini, which are usually cooked, make delicious salad ingredients when used raw. Never overcook vegetables to be served in a salad. They must be neither soft nor limp. Drain them immediately they are cooked. Both raw and cooked vegetables should be chilled and crisp. If you want to use leftover buttered vegetables in a salad, dip them in hot water or in hot meat stock to remove the butter, then drain and chill thoroughly.

Use your imagination in combining salad vegetables. Remember that no vegetable salad is perfect unless the ingredients harmonize in colour, flavour, and texture.

81. Tossed Vegetable Salad, Rancher's Style

1 small lettuce
*½ cucumber, peeled and thinly
  sliced*
8 radishes, thinly sliced
1 tomato, cut in wedges
3 spring onions and tops, sliced
½ pint soured cream
¼ lb. small curd cottage cheese
¼ teaspoon salt
Pepper, garlic salt, and paprika

Although this salad starts out as a regular mixed vegetable salad, it ends up with a different flavour. Instead of tossing with a French dressing, you coat the greens with a cottage cheese and soured cream mixture.

Tear the lettuce into small chunks and arrange in a salad bowl with the cucumber, radishes, tomato, and onions. Beat the soured cream with the cottage cheese and salt and add pepper, garlic salt, and paprika to taste. Pour over lettuce mixture and toss. Makes 6 to 8 servings.

82. Mexican Salad Bowl

4 slices bread, cut in ½-inch
  cubes
1 tablespoon butter or margarine
1 clove garlic, minced or
  mashed
¼ pint sliced celery
¼ pint finely sliced onion,
  separated into rings
½ green pepper, sliced
¼ pint shredded carrots
½ lb. diced boiled potatoes
1 medium-sized lettuce
4 tablespoons salad or olive oil
½ gill cider vinegar
1 teaspoon salt
Pepper to taste
1½ teaspoons caster sugar
1 teaspoon chilli powder
¼ teaspoon crumbled dried
  oregano
1 medium-sized avocado
Juice of 1 lemon or lime
¼ pint stuffed green olives

Garlic croûtons add crunchy bits of flavour to this mixed vegetable salad
tossed with a chilli-seasoned dressing.

Fry bread cubes in fat with the garlic until bread is golden brown. Drain
on paper towelling. Mix the celery, onion, green pepper, carrots, potatoes, and the croûtons lightly together. Heap in a salad bowl lined with
lettuce leaves. Blend the salad oil with the vinegar, salt, pepper, sugar,
chilli powder, and oregano. Pour over salad and toss lightly. Garnish
the top with slices of avocado sprinkled with lemon or lime juice and
with stuffed olives cut in half. Makes 8 servings.

83. Mixed Vegetable Salad

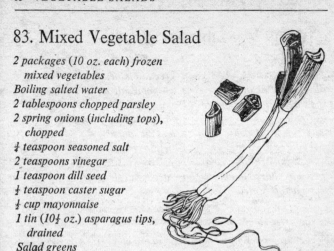

2 packages (10 oz. each) frozen
  mixed vegetables
Boiling salted water
2 tablespoons chopped parsley
2 spring onions (including tops),
  chopped
¼ teaspoon seasoned salt
2 teaspoons vinegar
1 teaspoon dill seed
½ teaspoon caster sugar
½ cup mayonnaise
1 tin (10½ oz.) asparagus tips,
  drained
Salad greens

Salads that can be made in advance are in demand for company as well
as family meals. This one is actually improved by chilling before being
served.

Cook the mixed vegetables in boiling salted water as directed on the
package, except allow about 2 minutes less cooking time than is specified.
Remove from heat, drain, and chill until about an hour before serving
time. Blend the parsley, spring onions, seasoned salt, vinegar, dill seed,
and sugar with the mayonnaise. Let stand in the refrigerator for at least
a half hour. Heap into a bowl lined with crisp greens. Arrange the
asparagus tips on top as a garnish. Makes 6 to 8 servings.

84. Bean Sprout and Water Chestnut Salad

Use fresh bean sprouts if you can find them – they are much crisper
than the tinned.

Clean sprouts well or drain the tinned ones. To each 2 cups of sprouts,
add ¼ cup sliced water chestnuts, ½ cup pineapple chunks, and ¼ cup
slivered green pepper. For the dressing, combine 1 cup mayonnaise with
1 teaspoon each soy sauce and curry powder. Mix the dressing through
the salad. Arrange salad in lettuce-lined bowl. Sprinkle toasted almonds
over the top. Makes 6 servings.

T – P.S.B. – C

85. Hearty Vegetable Salad

1 small cauliflower
Boiling salted water
¼ gill French dressing
2 cups shredded raw cabbage
10 oz. frozen peas
    or 1½ cups fresh peas,
    cooked
¼ lb. fresh spinach, shredded
¼ cup finely minced onion
1 small carrot, grated
1 cup cooked frozen or fresh small
    green lima beans
¼ teaspoon salt
Pepper to taste
¼ pint each French dressing
    and mayonnaise
10 lettuce cups
Paprika to taste
1 cup sliced celery

For eye appeal you vary the shape of the nine vegetables in this salad:
some you cut in shreds or slices; others stay whole.

Cook cauliflower in boiling salted water until barely tender. Drain and
let cool. Separate into flowerets, and marinate in the ½ gill French dressing, turning the cauliflowerets so that they are well coated with dressing. Chill. Toss the cabbage lightly with the peas, spinach, onion, carrot,
celery, lima beans, salt, and pepper to taste. Blend together the French
dressing and mayonnaise and toss with the mixed vegetables, including
the cauliflowerets. Pile into a lettuce-lined bowl and sprinkle with paprika. Makes 10 servings.

86. Tossed Cauliflower Salad

1 medium-sized head of cauli-
    flower
¼ pint French dressing
1 small avocado
½ cup sliced stuffed green olives
3 tomatoes, cut in eighths
2 oz. Roquefort cheese,
    crumbled
Crisp salad greens

Separate cauliflower into flowerets. Cover with iced water and chill 1
hour. Drain. Chop cauliflower coarsely. Sprinkle with the French dressing and let stand 2 hours. Just before serving, dice avocado and add to
salad along with olives, tomatoes, and cheese. Toss lightly. Serve on
crisp salad greens. Makes 8 servings.

87. Mexican Fiesta Salad

1 medium-sized lettuce
1 large avocado
4 tomatoes, peeled and diced
1 green pepper, seeded and
    chopped
1 small onion, finely chopped
4 rashers bacon
1½ teaspoons chilli powder
½ teaspoon salt
4 tablespoons cider vinegar

The name of this vegetable salad is suggested by its gay colours and the hot chilli dressing.

Line a salad bowl with lettuce torn into small pieces. Cut avocado in half lengthwise. Stone, peel, and slice. Arrange slices petal-like around the edge of the salad bowl. Pile diced tomatoes in the centre. Sprinkle with green pepper and onion. Fry bacon until crisp and crumble over all. Stir chilli powder and salt into bacon drippings. Stir in vinegar and pour at once over the salad. Serve immediately. Makes 6 to 8 servings.

88. Brussels Sprout Slaw

2 lb. Brussels sprouts
2 eggs
¼ pint soured cream
2 tablespoons melted butter or
    margarine
3 tablespoons vinegar
1¼ teaspoons salt
Pepper

Wash and trim sprouts, removing the outside leaves. Place sprouts in iced water to crisp. Drain thoroughly and cut crosswise in slices ⅛ inch thick. Chill. Beat the eggs in a saucepan with the soured cream and fat. Bring vinegar to a boil. Stirring constantly, pour the hot vinegar gradually into egg mixture. Still stirring, cook slowly until mixture is hot, but do not boil. Remove from heat, add salt and pepper to taste, then chill well.

When dressing is cold, pour over sliced sprouts and toss lightly. Chill until ready to serve. Makes 6 to 8 servings.

89. Fruit–Vegetable Salad Plate

¼ pint soured cream
¼ pint finely chopped chutney
2 tablespoons mayonnaise
¼ to ½ teaspoon Tabasco
Crisp lettuce leaves
1 pint cottage cheese
Few drops yellow food colouring
  (optional)
Choice of fruits and vegetables

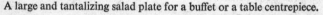

A large and tantalizing salad plate for a buffet or a table centrepiece.

To make the dressing, combine soured cream with chutney, mayonnaise, and Tabasco to taste. Refrigerate until time to serve. Arrange lettuce leaves on a large salad plate or platter. Add a little yellow food colouring to the cottage cheese if you wish. Mound in the centre of salad plate or platter.

  Arrange fruits and vegetables around the outside of the plate or platter – pineapple slices, banana chunks, fresh or tinned pear quarters, apple wedges, avocado slices, asparagus spears, tomato wedges, and cucumber slices. Pass the dressing separately. Makes 6 to 8 servings.

90. Brussels Sprout Salad

1½ lb. Brussels sprouts
Boiling salted water
¼ pint mayonnaise
2 tablespoons chopped ripe
  olives
6 tablespoons chilli sauce
1 tablespoon chopped onion

1 tablespoon vinegar
½ teaspoon minced parsley
Pinch of salt
1 hard-boiled egg, chopped
1 cos lettuce
1 tablespoon sliced pimiento

The type of dressing you use for coating crab, shrimp, or lobster salad suits a Brussels sprout salad equally well.

Cook Brussels sprouts in a large amount of boiling salted water until tender. Drain and chill. For the dressing mix the mayonnaise with the chopped olives, chilli sauce, onion, vinegar, parsley, salt, and chopped egg. Chill. Cut Brussels sprouts into ¼- to ½-inch thick slices. Add the dressing and mix lightly. Pile into a bowl lined with cos lettuce and garnish with pimiento. Makes 6 servings.

91. Oriental Vegetable Salad

¼ gill salad
  or olive oil
3 tablespoons tarragon vinegar
¼ gill tomato ketchup
2 tablespoons caster sugar
1 tablespoon lemon juice
¼ teaspoon salt
¼ teaspoon paprika
Pinch of garlic salt
¼ lb. fresh spinach

1 small tin (6 oz.) bamboo
  shoots
1 small tin (6 oz.) water
  chestnuts
1 medium-sized tin (18 oz.)
  bean sprouts
1 hard-boiled egg
2 tablespoons toasted sesame
  seeds or crisp, crumbled bacon

Toasted sesame seeds, bamboo shoots, and water chestnuts give an Oriental air to this salad. The sharp dressing sets off the mild-flavoured vegetables.

Gradually stir salad oil into vinegar. Add the ketchup, sugar, lemon juice, salt, paprika, and garlic salt, and stir thoroughly. Chill. Tear spinach into small pieces in salad bowl. Thinly slice bamboo shoots and water chestnuts, and place alternately with bean sprouts on a bed of spinach. Stir dressing and pour over salad. Sieve egg over salad and sprinkle with toasted sesame seeds or crumbled crisp bacon. Makes 6 servings.

92. Raw Cauliflower Salad

1 small head cauliflower, thinly
  sliced
3 unpeeled red apples, diced
1 cup sliced celery
3 small spring onions, sliced
3–4 tablespoons chopped
  parsley, or 1 small bunch
  watercress, chopped

1 clove garlic
¼ teaspoon salt
¼ gill red wine vinegar
½ gill salad or olive oil
Pepper to taste

Chill cauliflower, apples, celery, onions, and parsley or watercress thoroughly so that they are very crisp. Rub salad bowl with cut clove of garlic and salt. Shake vinegar, oil, and pepper vigorously in a tightly covered jar. Pour over salad and toss lightly. Makes 6 servings.

93. Italian Appetizer Salad

1 small head cauliflower
1 each medium-sized lettuce,
    escarole, and curly endive
1 lb. each sliced runner beans,
    kidney beans, and garbanzos
2 or 3 spring onions, chopped
6 hard-boiled eggs, sliced
¼ pint olive oil

¼ pint vinegar
1½ teaspoons salt
¼ teaspoon pepper
2 tomatoes, sliced
1 tin (2¼ oz.) sliced ripe olives
1 or 2 tins (2 oz. each)
    anchovies (rolled or fillets)

This salad, in a way, combines *antipasto* with salad greens. More than an 'appetizer', it deserves an important place in the menu.

Tear cauliflower into flowerets and parboil until just slightly tender; drain. Mix the greens, three kinds of beans, spring onions, and 4 of the eggs in a salad bowl. Toss with dressing made with oil, vinegar, salt, and pepper. Garnish top with tomato slices, remaining egg slices, olives, and anchovies. Serve immediately. Makes 10 to 12 servings.

NOTE : If garbanzos are not available, substitute cold boiled corn kernels.

94. Asparagus Salad

2 lb. asparagus
¼ pint soup stock or bouillon
¼ teaspoon salt
2 or 3 onion slices
¼ pint French dressing
1 small crisp lettuce
1 tablespoon chopped parsley
Fresh ground black pepper
Paprika to taste

Snap the tough lower ends off asparagus. Trim and wash stalks. Bring the soup stock or bouillon to a boil. Add salt and onion slices. Cook the asparagus in the seasoned stock until just tender. Carefully remove asparagus from the cooking liquid. Drain and arrange in a shallow dish. Pour over it a well-seasoned French dressing. Turn occasionally while cooling. When well chilled, arrange the stalks on shredded lettuce on individual salad plates. Sprinkle with freshly ground black pepper, paprika, and chopped parsley. If desired, arrange an anchovy strip or two over each portion of asparagus, and garnish each salad plate with tomato wedges and ripe or green olives. Makes 6 servings.

95. Marinated Artichokes

6 medium-sized globe
    artichokes
Boiling salted water
¼ pint olive or salad oil
5 cloves garlic, minced or
    mashed

3 tablespoons chopped fresh
    parsley
¼ cup lemon juice
¼ teaspoon salt
Dash of pepper
Chicory or other salad greens

Wash artichokes thoroughly under running water. Cut off stems and remove coarse outer leaves. Also cut about 1 inch off the tops, cutting straight across with a sharp knife. Set in a large saucepan with stem ends down. Cover with boiling water. Cover pan and cook until tender, 30 minutes to 1 hour, depending on the size of the artichokes. Drain well and spread apart the leaves slightly. Combine the oil with garlic, parsley, lemon juice, salt, and pepper. Pour this mixture over the artichokes, and stir them gently in this marinade, until the leaves are well coated. Return artichokes to the pan and simmer them for 10 minutes in the oil mixture. Let stand at room temperature at least 1 hour before serving. Arrange on individual salad plates garnished with blades of chicory. Makes 6 servings.

96. Sliced Cucumber and Onion Salad

3 medium-sized cucumbers
2 tablespoons salt
1½ quarts iced water
1 sweet onion
2 tablespoons salad or olive oil
2 tablespoons vinegar
Freshly ground pepper to taste

Cucumbers appear in a new guise here: they're sliced the long way with a vegetable peeler, so that each long paper-thin slice is rimmed with green peel.

With a vegetable peeler, slice unpeeled cucumbers lengthwise into very thin slices. Soak in salted, iced water in the refrigerator for at least 1 hour. Drain off all but 2 tablespoons of water. Peel onion, slice thinly, and separate into rings. Toss with the cucumber slices. Sprinkle salad or olive oil, vinegar, and pepper over all, and toss until vegetables are well coated with dressing. Serve immediately. Makes 6 to 8 servings.

97. Celeriac Salad Bowl

3 lb. (about 4 medium-sized)
   celeriac roots
½ pint diced celery
2 oz. chopped walnuts
2 tablespoons seedless raisins
2 tablespoons minced chives
2 tablespoons finely chopped
   green pepper
2 tablespoons stuffed green
   olives, cut in halves

1½ gills mayonnaise
1 teaspoon salt
¼ teaspoon Tabasco
2 tablespoons tarragon vinegar
Dash freshly ground pepper
Escarole or chicory
½ pint soured cream
Paprika to taste

This hearty salad looks like potato salad, but the white cubes are celeriac.
Other ingredients include walnuts, raisins, and celery.

Scrub celeriac roots. Place in a saucepan, cover with boiling water, cover
and simmer about 25 or 30 minutes, until tender. Drain, cool, peel, and
dice. Combine with celery, nuts, raisins, chives, green pepper, and olives.
Dress with mayonnaise blended with salt, Tabasco, vinegar, and
pepper. Chill. Mound salad on a bed of crisp escarole or chicory in a
salad bowl. Swirl soured cream on top and dust with paprika. Makes 8
servings.

98. Yogurt Cucumber Salad

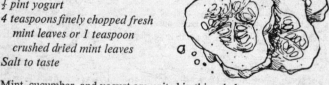

2 medium-sized cucumbers
½ pint yogurt
4 teaspoons finely chopped fresh
   mint leaves or 1 teaspoon
   crushed dried mint leaves
Salt to taste

Mint, cucumber, and yogurt are united in this salad.

Peel cucumbers and slice very thinly. Blend yogurt with mint leaves
and salt (add a touch of fresh garlic if desired). Toss cucumbers with
yogurt dressing. Chill at least 1 hour before serving. Makes 4 or 5 servings.

99. Celery Victor

2 small hearts of celery
1 medium-sized onion
1 pint bouillon or chicken stock
¼ pint well-seasoned French dressing
Watercress or shredded lettuce
Coarsely ground black pepper
Anchovy fillets and pimiento strips
Tomatoes and ripe olives (optional)

Chef Victor Hirtzler of the St Francis Hotel in San Francisco first originated this now classic salad in the early 1900s.

Wash celery, trim the root end, and cut off all but the smallest leaves. Peel and slice onion. Put whole celery hearts and sliced onion in a shallow pan. Cover with bouillon. Cover and cook until tender, about 15 minutes. Let cool in stock. Remove hearts, cut in half lengthwise, and place in a shallow dish. Pour French dressing over (a garlic-flavoured French dressing made with wine vinegar is especially good), and chill several hours.

To serve, drain off most of dressing and place celery on a bed of watercress or shredded lettuce. Sprinkle with pepper and garnish with anchovy fillets and pimiento strips. Quartered tomatoes and ripe olives may be used for extra garnish. Makes 4 servings.

100. Green and Gold Salad

3 cups boiled peas
2 oz. diced Cheddar cheese
3 tablespoons minced onion
¼ pint French dressing
1 tablespoon prepared mustard
Salad greens

To accompany this hearty luncheon salad, you might serve cold sliced meat or meat loaf, sliced tomatoes, devilled eggs, and hot rolls and butter.

Toss the peas, cheese, and onion lightly together. Pour in the French dressing, mixed with the mustard, and toss lightly. Chill. Spoon into a salad bowl lined with salad greens. Makes 6 servings.

101. Frosted Cauliflower Salad

1 head cauliflower
3 tablespoons wine vinegar
6 tablespoons olive oil
¼ teaspoon each salt and pepper
1 small clove garlic
2 avocados
2 ripe tomatoes
1 onion, finely chopped
Salt to taste

Mashed avocado, well seasoned, may be used to advantage to decorate a whole head of cauliflower which has been cooked just until tender and then chilled.

Cook whole head of cauliflower in salted water just until tender and no longer. Chill. Shake the vinegar with the oil, salt and pepper. Drop in garlic and let stand in dressing until just before using. Peel, stone, and mash avocados, peel and dice tomatoes, and combine with chopped onion. Add salt to taste and whip together until fluffy. Place chilled cauliflower in a salad bowl. Garnish with crisp salad greens. Pour oil and vinegar dressing over cauliflower, then frost with avocado and tomato mixture. Makes 6 or more servings, depending on size of the cauliflower.

102. Pea Salad

1½ cups boiled green peas
1 cup sliced celery
3 hard-boiled eggs, coarsely
  chopped
¼ pint mayonnaise
4 oz. coarsely chopped salted
  peanuts
3 tomatoes, sliced

Chopped salted peanuts top this colourful mixed vegetable salad.

Combine peas, celery, and chopped egg. Chill. To serve, spoon pea mixture on 6 salad plates. Drop spoonfuls of mayonnaise over each salad. Sprinkle with chopped peanuts, and garnish with tomato slices. Makes 6 servings.

103. Tarragon Cucumbers

2 medium-sized cucumbers
1 teaspoon salt
4 tablespoons fruit syrup from tinned apricots
About 2 tablespoons tarragon vinegar
1 teaspoon caster sugar
½ teaspoon fresh tarragon
or ¼ teaspoon dried tarragon
¼ teaspoon freshly ground black pepper
Salad greens
Sliced cucumber for garnish

A touch of tarragon and sweetening makes this salad unusually refreshing. If you haven't syrup from tinned apricots on hand, you can substitute peach or pear syrup.

Peel cucumbers. Slice very thinly into a bowl. (The slicing section of a grater is a good utensil.) Sprinkle salt over cucumbers. Place a weight on top of cucumbers. Allow to stand at room temperature for 6 to 8 hours. Occasionally drain off the juice that collects. Combine apricot syrup, vinegar, sugar, tarragon, and pepper. Taste and add a little more vinegar if dressing is too sweet. About 1 hour before serving, pour dressing over cucumbers. Toss lightly. Place in refrigerator to chill thoroughly. At serving time, turn cucumbers into a chilled shallow salad bowl lined with crisp salad greens. Garnish, if you wish, with a row of sliced unpeeled cucumber. Makes about 4 servings.

104. Near East Salad with Yogurt–Mint Dressing

½ pint each boiled green beans, peas, and diced or sliced carrots
1 cup thinly sliced unpeeled cucumbers
Crisp salad greens
Salt to taste
½ pint yogurt
4 tablespoons light cream
1 tablespoon finely chopped fresh mint leaves

Chill vegetables thoroughly. Arrange in separate stacks on 4 individual salad plates or in shallow bowls lined with crisp salad greens. Sprinkle lightly with salt. Blend yogurt with cream, and spoon on top of each salad. Sprinkle with the chopped fresh mint leaves. Makes 4 servings.

105. Dilled Green Pea Salad

1¼ lb. frozen peas
3 tablespoons salad oil
1–2 tablespoons lemon juice
¾ teaspoon dill weed
¼ teaspoon basil
1 whole clove garlic
Salt and pepper to taste
1 cup thinly sliced celery
Lettuce as required
Hard-boiled egg slices

Cook peas as directed on package. Drain, reserving ⅓ cup of the cooking water. Combine peas, the reserved cooking water, salad oil, lemon juice, dill weed, basil, garlic, salt and pepper. Chill. Discard garlic. Toss with celery. Serve from a lettuce-lined bowl. Decorate with the slices of egg. Makes 6 servings.

106. Marinated Green Bean Salad

2 tins (1 lb. each) kidney beans
2 tins (about 1 lb. each)
* whole green beans*
2 tins (about 1 lb. each)
* yellow wax beans*
2 tins (about 1 lb. each)
* garbanzos*
2 large green peppers, cut into
* thin rings*
Crisp cos lettuce leaves

1 large fresh red pepper, cut
* into thin rings*
5 medium-sized sweet salad
* onions, cut into thin rings*
1 cup sliced pimiento-stuffed
* olives*
1 tin (4 oz.) pimientos, diced
1½ gills each salad oil and white
* vinegar*
2 oz. caster sugar

This bean salad is full of flavour, crisp and light. For quickest preparation, use high quality tinned green and wax beans, but for best flavour, use boiled fresh beans if they're in season.

Turn thoroughly drained kidney beans, green beans, wax beans, and garbanzos into a large container for marinating. Add green and red peppers and onions. Sprinkle with olive slices and pimiento bits, reserving a few for garnish. Mix all lightly. Shake together in a covered jar the salad oil, vinegar, and sugar. Pour over bean mixture. Cover and marinate in refrigerator at least 6 hours before serving. At serving time, line a large wooden salad bowl with lettuce leaves. Turn in bean mixture. Garnish with reserved sliced olives and pimiento. Makes 20 servings.

107. Hot Beans and Bacon

1 lb. fresh green beans, cut up
or 1 tin (1 lb.) cut green
beans, drained
1 teaspoon salt
Dash of pepper
4 tablespoons salad oil
3 tablespoons tomato ketchup
2 tablespoons vinegar
¼ pint halved radishes
2 rashers crisply fried bacon

Chilled fresh radishes add sharpness and colour to this hot bean salad. Cook fresh beans in boiling salted water until tender, about 15 minutes. Drain. Mix the salt with the pepper, oil, ketchup, and vinegar. Pour dressing over hot beans and radishes, and toss. Crumble bacon over top. Serve hot. Makes 4 servings.

108. Frosted Green Bean Salad

1½ gills salad or olive oil
6 tablespoons vinegar
Salt and pepper to taste
2 lb. boiled green beans, split
lengthwise
1 bunch of spring onions,
sliced ¼ inch thick
8 hard-boiled eggs
6 tablespoons mayonnaise
4 teaspoons vinegar
2 teaspoons prepared mustard
8 rashers crisply fried bacon

This outstanding dish can double as salad and vegetable at a barbecue or buffet supper.

Shake the oil with the vinegar, and salt and pepper to taste. Pour over the green beans and onions and chill for several hours. Just before serving, chop the eggs and mix with mayonnaise, vinegar, and mustard. Crumble in the bacon and add salt to taste. Spoon egg topping over beans. Makes 8 servings.

109. Kidney Bean Salad

2 tins (1 lb. each) kidney
   beans, drained
1 cup sliced celery
1 green pepper, chopped
1 dill pickled cucumber, diced
¼ pint olive oil
¼ pint red wine vinegar
3 tablespoons each chopped
   parsley and spring onions
½ clove garlic, mashed or
   minced

1 tablespoon capers
1 teaspoon each minced fresh
   basil and tarragon
½ teaspoon chilli powder
1 teaspoon caster sugar
Few drops Tabasco
½ teaspoon salt
Salad greens, sliced radishes,
   tomato wedges
Freshly ground pepper

Tender and mild kidney beans, in combination with crisp vegetables and a sharp dressing, make a hearty salad.

Mix the kidney beans with the celery, green pepper, and dill pickle. Chill. Just before serving, combine olive oil, wine vinegar, parsley, spring onions, garlic, capers, basil, tarragon, chilli powder, sugar, Tabasco, and salt. Pour over salad mixture, then toss together gently. Arrange mixture on salad greens and garnish with sliced radishes and tomato wedges. Grind black pepper over salad before serving. Makes 8 servings.

110. Sweet–Sour Kidney Bean Cabbage Slaw

1 tin (1 lb.) kidney beans
2 cups shredded cabbage
½ gill chopped sweet pickles
½ gill sliced spring onions
2–3 oz. sultanas

½ teaspoon celery seed
3–4 tablespoons chilli sauce
¼ pint mayonnaise
Salt to taste

This is a tasty, one-dish substitute for a crisp cabbage cole slaw and a baked bean casserole. Try it served with hot dogs or grilled ham slices.

Drain and chill kidney beans. Toss together with cabbage, sweet pickles, onions, sultanas, celery seed, and a dressing made by combining the chilli sauce and mayonnaise. Salt to taste. Makes 6 servings.

111. Salami and Bean Salad

1 clove garlic (optional)
2 sprigs parsley, minced
½ small onion, chopped fine
1 small lettuce, torn in bits
1 tomato, cut in small pieces
¼ cup tinned kidney beans
Salt and pepper
4 thin slices salami
French dressing

Whether or not you rub your salad bowl with garlic depends on the strength of the salami you are using in this salad. Use wine vinegar in your French dressing to add extra zip.

Rub salad bowl with cut clove of garlic, if desired. Combine parsley, onion, lettuce, tomato, and kidney beans in salad bowl and sprinkle with salt and pepper. Cut salami in long thin strips and toss into salad. Pour French dressing over and toss thoroughly. Makes 4 servings.

112. Dried Bean Salad

2 cups dried beans
2½ pints water
2 teaspoons salt
¼ pint red wine vinegar
1 cup sliced celery
½ cup chopped spring onions
*   and tops*
½ cup chopped green pepper
6–8 lettuce cups

Cooked beans are chilled for this mixed vegetable salad. Vinegar blends with the sauce for a slightly tart dressing.

Wash the beans, then place in a large saucepan with the water. Cover, bring to the boil, and cook 2 minutes. Remove from heat and let soak 1 hour before cooking again. Add the salt, bring to the boil, and cook 2 hours, or until tender. Drain the beans and stir in the vinegar. Chill. To serve, add the celery, spring onions and tops, and green pepper. Mix lightly. Serve in lettuce cups. Makes 6 to 8 servings.

113. Lima Bean Salad

1½ packages (10 oz. each) frozen
   baby lima beans
1 cup sliced celery
1 dill-pickled cucumber, diced
4 spring onions and tops, chopped
¾ lb. bologna, cut in strips 1 inch
   long and ¼ inch thick

¼ pint soured cream
3–4 tablespoons mayonnaise
2 tablespoons lemon juice
2 teaspoons horseradish
   mustard
Crisp salad greens for garnish

Cook beans in boiling salted water 16 to 18 minutes, or until tender.
Drain and chill. Combine the chilled limas, celery, dill pickle, onions,
and bologna. Blend the soured cream with the mayonnaise, lemon
juice, and horseradish mustard until smooth. Pour dressing over lima
bean mixture, toss, and chill. When ready to serve, line 8 individual
plates with crisp salad greens. Spoon salad on greens. Makes 8 servings.

NOTE: When frozen baby lima beans are not available, you can make a
bean salad by the same recipe, using boiled small dried beans.

114. Full Meal Salad

1 package (10 oz.) frozen
   boiled lima beans
1 clove garlic, minced or
   mashed
¼ pint tart French dressing
1 teaspoon dry mustard
¼ teaspoon paprika
¼ teaspoon mixed dried herbs

Salt
3 spring onions and tops, sliced
4 radishes, sliced
1 to 1½ cups ham strips
2 oz. shredded Cheddar cheese
Leaves from lettuce heart
Mayonnaise

Lima beans, marinated in well-seasoned French dressing, make a flavourful salad base for ham and cheese strips. If not available, substitute any
boiled small dried beans.

Mix limas with garlic, French dressing, mustard, paprika, herbs, and
salt to taste. Chill. Toss lima beans with the onions, radishes, and ham
and cheese strips. Spoon into a bowl lined with lettuce leaves, and garnish with mayonnaise. Makes 4 servings.

115. Mushroom and Lima Bean Salad

*1 package (10 oz.) frozen lima
   beans*
*8 sliced fresh mushrooms or 1
   tin (4 oz.) sliced mushrooms,
   drained*
1 large onion, chopped
*1 tablespoon chopped fresh
   parsley*
¼ teaspoon oregano

4 tablespoons wine vinegar
3 tablespoons olive oil
*1 clove garlic, minced or
   mashed*
½ teaspoon salt
¼ teaspoon celery salt
¼ teaspoon pepper
Onion rings

Here lima beans benefit from a chilling in a spicy French dressing marinade. When not available, substitute any boiled small dried beans.

Cook lima beans according to package directions until tender. Drain, rinse under cold running water, and drain thoroughly again. Toss together with mushrooms, onion, parsley, and oregano.

   In a covered jar or container, shake the vinegar with the olive oil, garlic, salt, celery salt, and pepper. Pour over bean mixture and toss thoroughly. Chill in refrigerator 1 to 2 hours. To serve, heap into casserole lined with crisp salad greens. Garnish with thinly sliced onion rings. Makes 4 servings.

116. Slaw à l'Anchois

4 tablespoons olive oil
*2 oz. anchovy fillets in olive
   oil*
4 tablespoons vinegar
1 clove garlic, thinly sliced
1 medium-sized head cabbage
*4 rashers bacon, fried until
   very crisp*

Heat olive oil over medium heat. Add can of anchovies, including oil in which they are packed. Add vinegar and stir with fork until anchovies break apart. Add thinly sliced garlic and let simmer over low heat for 5 minutes.

   Shred cabbage into long, thin shreds. Pour hot dressing over. Mix and divide into individual servings. Crumble bacon over each serving. Makes 4 to 6 servings.

117. Walnut Cabbage Salad

1 small cabbage
1 avocado, cubed
1 carrot, grated
4–5 oz. chopped walnuts
4 spring onions, sliced
Garlic salt to taste
¼ pint mayonnaise
½ tablespoon prepared mustard
Juice of 1 lemon

This is a colourful cabbage salad with the yellow-green of avocado, the orange of carrots, the bright green of crisp onions, plus the additional crispness of walnut pieces.

Finely shred cabbage and mix with avocado, carrot, walnuts, onions, and garlic salt. Blend mayonnaise with mustard, and lemon juice, then add to vegetables and toss. Makes 6 servings.

118. California Slaw

1 small cabbage
2 tart apples, chopped
1 medium-sized onion, minced
2 pimientos, minced
3 hard-boiled eggs
¼ teaspoon salt
½ tablespoon caster sugar
1 teaspoon dry mustard
1 tablespoon butter, melted
4 tablespoons vinegar
¼ pint cream, whipped

A good choice for a quiet family dinner, this slaw would be equally at home at a party buffet. The dressing is based on hard-boiled egg yolks, beaten smooth and folded into whipped cream.

Shred cabbage and combine with apples, onion, and pimientos. Rub yolks of eggs to a paste and add salt, sugar, mustard, and butter. Mix well. Slowly add vinegar, beating thoroughly. Fold in cream. Combine with cabbage mixture and garnish with sliced egg whites and parsley. Makes 6 servings.

119. Lemon Slaw

6 cups finely shredded white
cabbage
2 unpeeled red apples, diced
¼ pint each chopped green
pepper and spring onions
1 teaspoon caster sugar
4 tablespoons dry white table
wine

This mixture of cabbage, red apple, green pepper, and onion is very colourful, crisp, and piquant.

Toss cabbage, apples, green pepper, and onions with sugar. Add wine, toss, and chill. Combine with this dressing: Mix together 3 hard-boiled egg yolks, 1 teaspoon dry mustard, 1 tablespoon sugar, 2 tablespoons salad oil, 1 teaspoon salt, pepper to taste, 1 teaspoon grated lemon peel, and ¼ pint lemon juice. Fold in ¼ pint whipping cream, beaten stiff. Makes 8 to 10 servings.

120. Grape Cole Slaw

1 medium cabbage, finely
shredded
1 carrot, shredded
6 oz. green grapes, seeded
3 oz. light raisins, plumped in
orange juice
Salt
1 tablespoon caster sugar
½ gill mayonnaise
2 tablespoons tarragon vinegar
¼ teaspoon curry powder

In five minutes you can assemble this fruity slaw. Grapes and raisins, plus a dash of curry, make it a children's light favourite. For extra eye appeal, serve it on a bed of crinkly dark green Savoy cabbage.

Combine the finely shredded cabbage with shredded carrots, grapes, and the raisins plumped in orange juice. Sprinkle with salt to taste, and sugar. For the dressing, blend the mayonnaise with the tarragon vinegar and curry powder. Add dressing to cabbage mixture and toss lightly. Garnish the bowl with lettuce leaves, if you wish. Makes 8 servings.

121. Tropical Cabbage Salad

1 medium-sized cabbage
4 oz. flaked coconut
1½ gills soured cream
2¼ tablespoons vinegar
¾ teaspoon salt
¼ teaspoon pepper
¼ tablespoon caster sugar
Toasted coconut
Paprika to taste

Finely shred cabbage. Add flaked coconut. Blend the soured cream with the vinegar, salt, pepper, and sugar. Toss lightly with cabbage and coconut. Sprinkle with toasted coconut and paprika. (To toast coconut, spread a thin layer on a baking sheet and toast in a 350° F. oven for 3 or 4 minutes, watching carefully and stirring when necessary.) Makes 6 to 8 servings.

122. Beetroot and Curry Salad

¼ pint vinegar
½ gill salad oil
1 teaspoon caster sugar
Salt, pepper, and curry powder
*   to taste*
1 tin (1 lb.) diced beetroot, drained
¼ pint chopped onion
4 lettuce cups

The strength of the curry powder you use determines the amount (about ½ teaspoon, or more to taste).

In a jar with a cover, mix vinegar, salad oil, sugar, salt, pepper, and curry powder. Shake well. Combine beetroot, onion, and dressing. Mix well, and let chill several hours. Spoon into lettuce cups. Makes 4 servings.

123. Mediterranean Salad

2 tablespoons olive oil
1 medium-sized onion
  finely chopped
1 medium-sized aubergine, peeled
  and cut in small cubes
1 teaspoon salt
4 oz. rice
½ pint water
1½ tablespoons tomato ketchup
2 green peppers

This stuffed pepper salad combines some unusual flavours. You might serve it with cold ham or tongue.

Heat the oil in a medium-sized saucepan. Add the onion and aubergine cubes. Cook for about 5 minutes, or until soft. Add the salt, rice, and water. Cover and cook over low heat until the rice is tender. Stir in the ketchup. Cut the peppers in halves, remove the seeds and veins, and fill with the rice mixture. Stand in a baking tin, and pour about ½ gill water in the bottom of the tin. Bake in a moderate oven (350°F.) for 30 to 40 minutes, or until the peppers are tender, but still firm. Chill. Serve cold, topped with mayonnaise sauce. Makes 2 to 4 servings.

MAYONNAISE SAUCE:
Combine ¼ pint mayonnaise with 2 tablespoons sweet pickle relish and 2 tablespoons lemon juice.

124. Green Pepper Ring Salad

Curly endive and shredded lettuce
2 green peppers, cut in thin rings
2 medium-sized onions, thinly
  sliced
¼ pint tart French dressing

You have to enjoy the crispness and sharpness of green pepper and onion rings to appreciate this combination.

Line 6 salad plates with endive and shredded lettuce. Arrange alternate rings of green pepper and onion on greens. Before serving, pour a little tart French dressing over each salad. Makes 6 servings.

125. Orange and Green Pepper Salad

Cut the peel from 6 oranges, so that all white is removed, and cut in slices ⅓ inch thick. Arrange in overlapping rows on a platter. Surround with lettuce leaves, and top with 1 sweet onion and 1 green pepper, sliced so thin they are transparent. (You'll need a sharp knife for this. Or, if you'd rather, just chop the onion and pepper very finely.) Arrange on top of the oranges. Sprinkle with about ½ pint French dressing, and chill thoroughly before serving. Makes 12 servings.

126. Aubergine Salad

1 medium-sized aubergine
2 spring onions, chopped
3 medium-sized fresh tomatoes,
  cut in cubes
¼ gill cider vinegar
3 tablespoons salad oil
1½ teaspoons salt
Freshly ground pepper to taste
½ teaspoon caster sugar
Lettuce as required

Here is an interesting new way to treat aubergine. Combined with bright red tomatoes, it makes a colourful and unusual salad. As an extra advantage, it's a salad that you can make ahead of time, then leave to marinate in the refrigerator for several hours.

Wash the aubergine and set it on a baking sheet without peeling it. Bake in a moderately hot oven (375° F.) for about 45 minutes, or until tender when pierced with a fork. Peel when it is cool enough to handle. Chill in your refrigerator. Cut the aubergine into cubes. Mix it with onion, tomatoes, vinegar, salad oil, salt, pepper, and sugar. Chill for several hours. Serve on lettuce. Makes 4 to 6 servings.

127. Hearts of Palm

Cut canned palm pieces in half lengthwise. Pour over them wine vinegar or red table wine and olive oil. Sprinkle with plenty of freshly ground pepper and garnish with pimiento slivers. Chill for a few hours before serving.

128. Brazilian Heart of Palm Salad

Arrange sliced lettuce on individual plates. Sprinkle with salt, pepper, a little lemon juice, and minced chives. Top each with half a peeled ripe tomato. Chop watercress, allowing 3 tablespoons (packed) for each serving, and mix with 1½ tablespoons chopped heart of palm and just enough French dressing to hold together (use 3 parts light salad oil to 1 part lemon juice, salt and pepper). Mound on top of each tomato and serve.

129. Water Chestnut Salad

Follow above recipe, but substitute water chestnuts for the hearts of palm.

130. Mushroom–Olive Salad

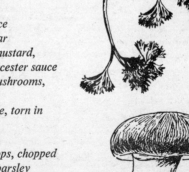

1 teaspoon salt
1 tablespoon water
1 clove garlic, minced
8 tablespoons salad oil
3 tablespoons vinegar
2 teaspoons lemon juice
1 teaspoon caster sugar
¼ teaspoon each dry mustard,
  rosemary, and Worcester sauce
1 tin (4 oz.) button mushrooms,
  drained
1 medium-sized lettuce, torn in
  shreds
¼ cup sliced celery
3 spring onions and tops, chopped
1 tablespoon minced parsley
¼ gill stuffed green olives, sliced

Dissolve salt in water; add garlic and let stand for at least 30 minutes; stir occasionally. Mix the salad oil with the vinegar, lemon juice, sugar, mustard, rosemary, Worcester sauce, and mushrooms. Strain garlic and add garlic water to dressing. Let stand 20 minutes. Remove mushrooms and arrange with lettuce, celery, onions, parsley, and olives in a bowl. Add dressing and toss lightly. Makes 6 servings.

131. Fresh Mushroom Salad

½ pint soured cream
1 tablespoon lemon juice
1 teaspoon each salt and sugar
¼ lb. mushrooms, thinly sliced
2 spring onions, sliced
1 medium-sized crisp lettuce
2 hard-boiled eggs, grated

Raw fresh mushrooms, sliced wafer-thin, add their distinctive flavour to this creamy, tart dressing that you spoon over wedges of head lettuce.

Mix soured cream with the lemon juice, salt, sugar, sliced mushrooms, and onions. Cut lettuce into quarters and arrange on 4 plates. Spoon over chilled dressing and sprinkle with grated egg. Makes 4 servings.

132. Continental Potato Salad

2 lb. new potatoes
1 teaspoon caster sugar
1 teaspoon salt
¼ teaspoon dry mustard
Freshly ground pepper
3 tablespoons vinegar
2 teaspoons caraway or dill seed
    (optional)
1 cucumber, sliced
About ¾ pint
    soured cream
Lettuce as required
Paprika or finely minced, sweet
    red pepper

A well-chilled, robust potato salad is always a favourite. Here is an especially good version.

Boil potatoes. Peel and slice thin. Mix sugar with the salt, mustard, pepper, vinegar, caraway or dill seed, cucumber, and soured cream. Combine with potatoes. Chill. Put in a lettuce-lined bowl, and sprinkle with paprika or red pepper. Makes about 6 servings.

133. Kohl Rabi Salad Niçoise

1 pint peeled, coarsely
shredded kohl rabi
¼ cup sliced radishes
3 tablespoons mayonnaise
1 teaspoon caster sugar
2 tablespoons each vinegar and
salad oil
½ teaspoon dry mustard
Salt and pepper to taste
3 or 4 lettuce cups
Paprika to taste

Toss kohl rabi and radishes with the mayonnaise mixed with the sugar, vinegar, salad oil, mustard, salt, and pepper. Chill for several hours. Serve in crisp lettuce cups, sprinkled with a little paprika. Makes 3 or 4 servings.

134. Hot Cheese–Potato Salad

4 cups peeled and cubed boiled
potatoes
2 hard-boiled eggs, chopped
½ cup sliced celery
4 tablespoons minced onion
2 tablespoons minced green pepper
4 tablespoons cider vinegar
1 teaspoon salt
1 teaspoon dry mustard
¼ teaspoon pepper
2 rashers bacon, diced
½ lb. shredded sharp Cheddar cheese

This interesting winter version of potato salad has a grilled Cheddar cheese topping. For a variation, add some sliced ripe olives.

In a large bowl, mix together the potatoes, eggs, celery, onion, and green pepper. Sprinkle with vinegar, salt, mustard, and pepper. Sauté bacon until crisp. Pour bacon dripping and crisp bacon over potato mixture and toss lightly. Turn into a shallow baking tin and sprinkle with cheese. Place under the grill until the cheese is bubbly. Makes 8 servings.

135. Curried Potato Salad

6 large potatoes
¼ pint tart French dressing
4 hard-boiled eggs, chopped
½ pint chopped onion
½ pint chopped celery
1 small green pepper, finely
    chopped
About ¾ pint mayonnaise
1 tablespoon curry powder
½ to ¾ teaspoon salt
Cos lettuce leaves

The day before, bake potatoes in a very hot oven (450°) about 1 hour or until tender. Remove skins when they are cool enough to handle. Cover and allow to cool completely. Slice potatoes into a large bowl. Sprinkle thoroughly with the French dressing. Cover and store in the refrigerator. Chop eggs, onion, celery, and green pepper. Store in separate containers in refrigerator. Blend ½ gill of the mayonnaise with the curry powder and salt; then stir in remaining mayonnaise to taste. Several hours before serving combine potatoes, eggs, onion, and celery. Fold mayonnaise into potato mixture and arrange in a bowl lined with lettuce leaves. Garnish with the chopped green pepper. Makes 16 servings.

136. French Potato Salad

The tart, peppery seasoning in this salad distinguishes it from the standard potato salads. Try this with steak in place of the traditional French fried potatoes.

Cook 8 small, round waxy potatoes in their skins until tender. Peel and slice thinly. Peel and slice very thinly one mild onion. Separate into rings. In a shallow dish place alternate layers of the sliced potatoes and onion rings. Salt and pepper each layer and sprinkle chopped parsley over it. Make French dressing with 2 tablespoons white wine vinegar and 3 tablespoons salad oil. Pour dressing over layers of potato and onion and refrigerate salad overnight. Turn mixture at least once to make sure salad is well coated with the dressing. Makes about 5 servings.

137. Hot Potato and Bacon Salad

8 medium-sized potatoes
  cooked and cut in ½-inch
  cubes
16 rashers bacon, fried and
  crumbled
½ pint chopped spring onions
  and tops
½ teaspoon salt
Dash of pepper

¾ pint of mayonnaise
1–2 tablespoons prepared
  mustard
2 tablespoons prepared horseradish
1 cup sliced celery
¼ cup finely chopped carrots
Paprika to taste

Mix the cubed potatoes with the crumbled bacon, onions, salt, and pepper. Combine the mayonnaise, mustard, and horseradish in a saucepan. Heat, stirring constantly, until sauce bubbles. Stir in the celery and carrots. Pour the hot sauce over potato mixture and toss lightly. Sprinkle paprika over top and serve immediately. Makes 8 generous servings.

138. Cottage Cheese–Potato Salad

8 oz. creamed cottage cheese
¼ pint mayonnaise
1 tablespoon lemon juice
1 teaspoon dry mustard
1–1½ teaspoons salt
1 saltspoon pepper
3 cups boiled, diced potatoes
¼ cup thinly sliced celery
2 tablespoons onions, finely
  chopped
1 tablespoon each chopped
  green pepper and chopped pimiento
Crisp salad greens

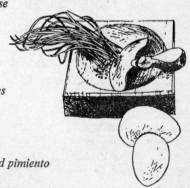

Potato salad has a different texture when bound together with a mayonnaise-cottage cheese mixture. Bits of green pepper and pimiento brighten its appearance.

Mix the cottage cheese with the mayonnaise, lemon juice, mustard, salt, and pepper. Lightly toss with potatoes, celery, onions, green pepper, and pimiento. Chill thoroughly. Serve in individual lettuce cups or in a salad bowl lined with greens. Makes 6 servings.

139. Tomatoes in Sweet–Sour Dressing

4 or 5 large, firm, ripe
  tomatoes
6 tablespoons red or white wine
  vinegar
3 tablespoons water
¼ tablespoon caster sugar
2 tablespoons finely chopped
  spring onions and tops
Freshly ground pepper

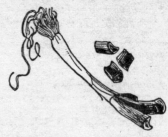

Here, the tang of wine vinegar contrasts with the sweetness of tomatoes.
Peel tomatoes and cut crosswise in thick slices. Arrange on a serving
platter. Mix together the vinegar, water, sugar, and chopped onions.
Pour over tomatoes. Grind pepper to taste over all. Chill at least 1 hour.
Makes 6 servings.

140. East Indian Salad

12 tomatoes, peeled
3¼ gills mayonnaise
1 tablespoon curry powder
2 teaspoons lemon juice
12 minced anchovies
¼ pint boiled shrimps
¼ pint olives, stoned
1 envelope (1 tablespoon)
  unflavoured gelatine
3 tablespoons cold water
Sprigs of parsley for garnish

These piquant stuffed tomatoes add an interesting touch to a holiday
buffet.

Scoop out centres from tomatoes, and turn upside down to drain. Combine mayonnaise, curry powder, lemon juice, anchovies, shrimps, and
olives. Soften gelatine in the cold water and melt over hot water. Add
gelatine to shrimp mixture. Spoon into tomatoes and chill thoroughly.
Garnish tops with parsley. Makes 12 servings.

141. Garlic Tomato Salad

Chilled, garlic-seasoned, sliced tomatoes are an especially good accompaniment for barbecued chops, steaks, or hamburgers. Scald and peel 5 large tomatoes. Cut in ⅛-inch-thick slices. Place a single layer of the sliced tomatoes on a platter.

To ¾ pint French dressing, add 1 or 2 cloves of garlic, mashed or minced. Pour some of the dressing mixture over tomatoes. Sprinkle with crushed oregano, salt, and pepper. Add another layer of tomato slices, and repeat dressing, oregano, salt, and pepper. Continue until all tomato slices are used. Cover platter with foil and chill for at least 3 hours. Makes 8 servings.

142. Bean Sprout–Stuffed Tomatoes

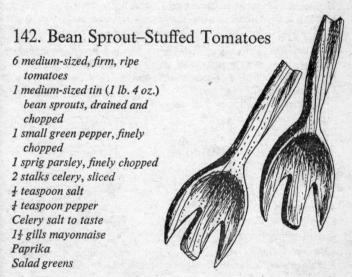

6 medium-sized, firm, ripe
  tomatoes
1 medium-sized tin (1 lb. 4 oz.)
  bean sprouts, drained and
  chopped
1 small green pepper, finely
  chopped
1 sprig parsley, finely chopped
2 stalks celery, sliced
½ teaspoon salt
¼ teaspoon pepper
Celery salt to taste
1½ gills mayonnaise
Paprika
Salad greens

Crisp celery and rather bland bean sprouts combine well with tomato to make a colourful salad.

Cut out stem end of tomatoes and scoop out the pulp, leaving firm shells. Chill. Drain off excess juice from pulp and combine with bean sprouts, green pepper, parsley, celery, salt, pepper, celery salt, and mayonnaise. Stuff tomato shells with salad mixture and shake paprika over top. Arrange on crisp greens. Makes 6 servings.

143. Stuffed Tomato Casserole Salad

2 cups diced boiled potatoes
1 cup small Swiss cheese cubes
1½ gills diced bologna
1 small onion, finely chopped
Salt and pepper to taste
¼ pint sharp French dressing
6 large tomatoes
Mayonnaise
Paprika
Lettuce as required

This is not the usual stuffed tomato salad. Cubes of Swiss cheese, bologna, and potato blend with the zippy onion seasoning.

In a large bowl, combine potatoes, Swiss cheese cubes, bologna, onion, salt, and pepper. Mix lightly with French dressing. Remove stem ends from tomatoes. With a sharp knife, slash from top half-way down each tomato, in about 6 places. Spread tomato open. Fill with potato mixture. Top with a spoonful of mayonnaise, and a dusting of paprika if desired. Serve in lettuce-lined individual casseroles. Makes 6 servings.

144. Tomato, Orange, and Anchovy Salad

4 firm, ripe tomatoes
4 oranges
Lettuce
4 oz. anchovy fillets
½ cup sliced stuffed olives
4 tablespoons olive oil
3 tablespoons wine vinegar
¼ teaspoon salt
Freshly ground pepper

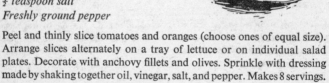

Peel and thinly slice tomatoes and oranges (choose ones of equal size). Arrange slices alternately on a tray of lettuce or on individual salad plates. Decorate with anchovy fillets and olives. Sprinkle with dressing made by shaking together oil, vinegar, salt, and pepper. Makes 8 servings.

145. Sliced Tomatoes with Mustard Dressing

½ pint cider vinegar
3 eggs
2–3 oz. caster sugar
2 tablespoons flour
1 teaspoon dry mustard
½ teaspoon salt

¼ teaspoon pepper
½ gill whipping cream
8 medium-sized, firm, ripe
 tomatoes
Shredded lettuce
½ tablespoon mustard seeds

Mustard – in powdered form in the dressing and as seeds on top – spices this tomato salad.

Heat vinegar to scalding. Beat eggs until blended. Mix together sugar, flour, and mustard and beat into the eggs. Stir in salt and pepper. Gradually add the hot vinegar to the egg mixture and beat until blended. Cook over low heat, stirring for 2 minutes. Cool. When ready to serve, whip cream and fold in. Peel and slice tomatoes. Arrange them on shredded lettuce on a large platter. Spoon dressing over the tomatoes and sprinkle mustard seeds over all. Makes 10 generous servings.

146. Sauerkraut–Stuffed Tomatoes

12 medium-sized, firm, ripe
 tomatoes
Salt and pepper to taste
6 tablespoons salad oil
3 tablespoons lemon juice
1 tablespoon caster sugar
¼ teaspoon paprika
1 saltspoon salt
1 large tin (1 lb. 13 oz.)
 sauerkraut
Cos lettuce or other crisp salad greens

The sharp acidity of sauerkraut makes an interesting flavour contrast to sun-sweet tomatoes in this salad.

Peel tomatoes, cut off stem end, and scoop out most of pulp, leaving a thick shell. Turn upside down to drain. Sprinkle the tomato cavities with salt and pepper to taste. Mix together the oil, lemon juice, sugar, paprika, and the salt. Pour dressing over sauerkraut and toss lightly. Spoon sauerkraut mixture into tomato cavities. Chill tomatoes for about 1 hour. Arrange stuffed tomatoes on salad greens. Makes 12 servings.

147. Vegetable Salad with Zucchini

1 small lettuce
1½ cups thinly sliced raw
   zucchini
¼ cup sliced celery
1 cup thinly sliced raw carrots
2 spring onions and tops,
   chopped
5 radishes, sliced
1 tablespoon chopped parsley
¼ teaspoon salt
¼ pint mayonnaise
3–4 tablespoons tarragon or wine
   vinegar

Crisp wheels of raw zucchini are tossed with other vegetables in this combination salad. If you wish, embellish the basic salad dressing with salad herbs.

Shred lettuce and toss with the zucchini, celery, carrots, onions and tops, radishes, and parsley. Sprinkle with salt. Mix together mayonnaise and vinegar and add. Toss thoroughly until vegetables are coated with dressing. Makes 6 servings.

1. Green salad, smörgasbord style (Recipe 1), presents a colourful
picture. Bowl of lettuce includes cos, leaf, curly endive, chicory. Other
ingredients are served separately, to be sprinkled on individual servings.
Toss greens with Piquant Dressing (Recipe 265) just before serving.

2. A tempting array of salad greens is available in today's markets.
Nine of the major kinds are shown here. For some salads, you'll want
to use a single kind; but when little or nothing is added to the greens,
a combination of two or more greens will give contrast in colours,
flavours, and textures. 1. Leaf Lettuce. Delicate taste; very tender,
fragile leaves, lightweight, closely crinkled; 2. Cos Lettuce. Brittle-crisp,
somewhat fibrous, clean-tearing; spicy-mild and juicy; 3. Oak Leaf
Lettuce. Mellow flavour, slight bite; soft, suede-like leaf; 4. Curly Endive.
Wiry, sharply feathered, wispy leaf; sprightly, rather bitter flavour;
5. Cabbage Lettuce. Mild, almost tasteless; pliable soft leaf; velvety
texture; 6. Watercress. Lively and spicy sweetness; sharp and biting;
fragile, petal-like leaves; 7. Webb's Wonder (sometimes called
Iceberg Lettuce). Brittle, very crisp; icy bite; watery taste; 8. Chicory.
Lively taste: rich, mildly acrid; waxen, crunchy spears; 9. Escarole
(Broad Leaf Endive). Sharp, slightly bitter; rough-textured, wiry,
leathery leaf.

3. 'Accessory' greens add an element of surprise and interest to a salad.
The twelve above are by no means an exhaustive collection. A tossed
green salad might include such ingredients as sorrel, Chinese cabbage,
or herbs fresh from the garden. 1. Leeks. Robust, strong aroma;
a mild, sweet, oniony flavour; 2. Fennel (Anise). Use stalk and feathery
top; liquorice flavour; 3. Spring Onions. Appetizing aroma,
sweet-onion piquancy; 4. Chives. Refined onion qualities; dainty and
refreshing fragrance; 5. Celery. Fragile tufts; nutty, spicy; sweet pungency;
6. Beet Tops. Young, firm leaves; mildly sour, salty; 7. Dandelion Greens.
Thin, arrowy leaf; tart-bitter taste; 8. Mustard Greens. Young,
fully frilled leaves; peppery-bitter; 9. Spinach. Tender young leaves;
sharp edges; clean, 'green' taste; 10. Nasturium Leaves. Peppery,
somewhat like watercress; 11. Mint. Fruity, refreshingly sweet scent;
fuzzy leaves; 12. Parsley. Acid-sweet, fresh, ferny-leafed, slightly tough.

4a. For this mixed green salad I have selected a variety of salad greens: cos and cabbage lettuce, curly endive, escarole, avocado slices for garnish. Toss torn greens with a distinctive dressing.

4b. Vegetable salad shown here combines kidney beans, cooked and chilled peas, asparagus, young broad beans, quartered tomatoes. Salad is arranged in lettuce cups, served with Thousand Island Dressing.

4c. Full-meal salad: shrimps, sliced celery, chopped egg, mixed with salad dressing or mayonnaise, lemon juice, salt, pepper, celery seed, shredded lettuce, egg slices, tomato, green pepper.

5a. Ingredients for Caesar Salad (Recipe 15) are shown here. This salad is invariably tossed at the table where guests can watch the host or hostess season and mix the greens. Crisp and flavourful cos lettuce leaves, torn into large pieces, always form the background of a Caesar Salad.

5b. Green Goddess salad (Recipe 22), with a lobster garnish, is an especially colourful and rich version of plain green salad. The creamy dressing may be used on many salads, both light and hearty.

5c. Grapefruit sections and avocado slices, arranged in an alternating pattern on a crisp bed of curly endive, are pleasing to the eye.

6a. Colour-flecked filling for iceberg lettuce: combine 3 oz. cream cheese with 3 tablespoons mayonnaise, 2 tablespoons each grated carrot, chopped tomato; 1 tablespoon each chopped green pepper, pimiento, onion; salt, paprika, pepper.

6b. Remove core from a large, firm head of lettuce. Hollow out a hole 5 inches deep in the centre of head. Stuff with cream cheese filling. Wrap with aluminium foil and chill for 6 hours. Cut in crosswise slices. Serve on a platter with olives and radishes mounted in the centre.

7a. Wedges of any crisp lettuce are served with a Thousand Island Dressing to which chopped beetroot was added for colour interest.

7b. Minced vegetable dressing (Recipe 267) ideally complements sliced tomatoes, cucumbers. This dressing is also good on lettuce wedges.

8a. Salad Buffet is fun to assemble and fun for the guests. The picture above doesn't begin to show all of the foods which could go on the buffet table. In addition to the mayonnaise and the cruets of oil and vinegar you might set on the table a variety of dressings and condiments. You might also add toasted sesame seeds, slivered bologna, smoked turkey, smoked oyster bits, or flaked tuna fish to the accompaniments, as available. Vegetable possibilities are almost unlimited, and you can branch out into fruit salads too. 1. Anchovies, Sardines; 2. Pickled Onions, Beets; 3. Artichoke Hearts, Pickled Mushrooms; 4. Lemons; 5. Salt and Pepper; 6. Mayonnaise; 7. Chopped Egg; 8. Flat Bread, French Bread, Rye Bread, Rye Wafers; 9. Jellied Tongue, Turkey, Ham, Salami, Beef; 10. Cream Cheese, Cheddar Cheese, Blue Cheese, Swiss Cheese, Parmesan Cheese; 11. Ripe Olives; 12. Iceberg Lettuce; 13. Oil and Vinegar; 14. Crisp Lettuce; 15. Cos Lettuce; 16. Escarole; 17. Curly Endive; 18. Carrots, Tomatoes, Onions, Cauliflower, Radishes; 19. Garlic Croutons; 20. Prawns; 21. Toasted Almonds; 22. Asparagus; 23. Green Olives; 24. Crumbled Bacon; 25. Smoked Salmon; 26. Crab.

8b. Antipasto Salad (Recipe 20) is arranged on a base of shredded cos lettuce and curly endive. Leaf lettuce forms border. Strips of antipasto ingredients are tuna chunks, pimiento strips, chopped spring onion, radish slices, chopped egg yolks and whites, green olive slices, anchovy fillets, chopped parsley.

9a. Wedges of hard-boiled eggs decorate Dilled Green Pea Salad (Recipe 105). Toasted cornbread squares are a delicious accompaniment.

9b. Mushroom and Lima Bean Salad (Recipe 115) is heaped in a large casserole lined with cos lettuce leaves.

9c. Lemon Slaw (Recipe 119) is colourful, and it tastes as good as it looks. Fresh lemon juice, plus a little grated lemon peel, gives the dressing a refreshing tang.

10a, 10b. Cobb Salad
(Recipe 172) has an
unusual flavour. Rich
with chicken, tomatoes,
hard-boiled eggs, Roquefort
cheese, and avocados, it is
a meal in itself.

10c. Dried Bean Salad (Recipe 112) would be a good choice for a winter
luncheon. As accompaniments, you might serve bouillon, bran muffins,
an assortment of cheese, and a platter of cold sliced meat loaf or
other cold meats.

11a. Chicken Salad Piquant (Recipe 161) has a flavourful low-calorie dressing that will please weight watchers – only about 2 calories per tablespoon.

11b. Mushroom-Olive Salad (Recipe 130) is tossed in a garlic-flavoured dressing. Celery, onions, and parsley give added texture contrasts.

11c. Three colourful party salads: Fruits frozen in sherry cream base (Recipe 229), avocados with pears and pineapple (Recipe 37), tomato with poached oyster and anchovy sauce (Recipe 182).

11d. Orange and cucumber slices are tucked among leaves of lettuce, and overlapping onion rings decorate the top. (Recipe 19).

12a. Chicken and avocado salad served on a Mexican plate presents a colourful picture. Avocado slices radiate above shredded crisp lettuce and slices of chicken. Garnish with grated cheese, sliced radishes, spring onions, and tomato wedges.

12b. Prawn salad with lemon dressing (Recipe 193) is served on watercress and embellished with tiny pickled beets and bright devilled eggs. Garnish with prawns or shrimps chilled with ice cubes.

13a. Grapefruit segments alternate with slices of ripe melon or papaya on a bed of crisp iceberg lettuce and watercress. Sliced hearts of palm and chopped ripe olives embellish this buffet salad. Ingredients used: 1 large grapefruit, 1 melon or papaya, 1 can (14 oz.) hearts of palm, and 12 stoned ripe olives.

13b. To make grapefruit segments, peel grapefruit down to meat in circular fashion, removing all of the outer skin and inside membrane. Slip knife down one side of dividing membrane, then continue along the membrane on the other side of segment so fruit drops out.

14a. Fruit plate of papaya, orange, banana, and pineapple slices is topped with papaya seed dressing (Recipe 269). Papaya seeds taste a little like capers. When not available substitute capers or poppy seeds. When papaya is not available the salad can be made with slices of ripe melon.

14b. A pear slicer cuts melons and papaya quickly. Remove blossom end from small fruit. Push slicer through. Peel with potato peeler.

15a. Papaya (or melon, Recipe 65) oranges, and avocados, drenched in an onion-flecked red chilli dressing have marinaded earlier in this same mixture.

15b. Star-shaped cavity in papaya is different from the round centre in most melons. Stuff with cream cheese mixture. (Recipe 66), then slice.

15c. To prepare half papaya, scoop out seeds with a table-spoon. They're easy to remove, as they tend to cling together.

16a. Avocado halves, filled with mandarin oranges and arranged on a bed of curly endive, are a good first course for a meal (Recipe 44).

16b. Ham and cheese rice salad (Recipe 205) is served in a casserole. It has the heartiness of an oven-baked casserole, but it is served crisp and cold. The Swiss cheese, ham, and dill make a mellow blend of flavours.

17a. Fruit and cottage cheese salad in cos lettuce leaves (Recipe 25) has a garnish of cantaloup and strawberries. It is served with an unusual mint-flavoured dressing.

17b. 17c. Casserole Salads: Above, a curry dressing gives a Far Eastern accent to rice salad (Recipe 203). Left, sultanas add glamour to a combination of kidney bean and cabbage in an extra-hearty slaw (Recipe 110).

18a, 18b. Frosted Salmon Mousse (Recipe 245) is a delicious luncheon entrée. The moulded salmon salad is flecked with sliced ripe olives and frosted with a pale green avocado-sour cream mixture.

19a. Washington Apple Salad (Recipe 213) is delicate and rather sweet. Cottage cheese and evaporated milk substitute for the more typical cream cheese and whipped cream.

19b. Tomato aspic ring, filled with avocado cubes which are sprinkled with salt and lemon juice, and surrounded by devilled hard-boiled eggs, could be the main course at a company luncheon. Serve it with French dressing to which chopped chives have been added.

20a. Cheese-filled fresh pineapple is cut in slices for serving. Cheese is softened with a little cream and mixed with chopped nuts and sliced maraschino cherries.

20b. To prepare pineapple, remove top and bottom; remove rind and cut out any remaining eyes. Use cylinder from a biscuit press to remove core. Pack cream cheese mixture into hollow centre; wrap in waxed paper and chill thoroughly. Cut into thick slices. Serve on leaves or greens.

21a. Lime-lemon-orange layered salad (Recipe 226) is an unusual combination of fruits and vegetables, with a sour cream layer in the centre. It is garnished with pineapple chunks, green-coloured maraschino cherries, and halved bananas coated with chopped peanuts.

21b. Double-decker pineapple-cherry salad (Recipe 228) has a thin layer of cream cheese sandwiched between the two fruit-flavoured layers. Mandarin oranges and cream balls rolled in coconut provide an attractive garnish.

22a. Sweet dark cherries, coarsely chopped pecans, and sliced pimiento-stuffed olives are moulded in orange jelly (Recipe 218).

22b. Orange cottage cheese tops pineapple slices (Recipe 79) for an attractive buffet salad plate. Dressing is served in hollowed-out pineapple shell.

22c. Slices of hard-boiled eggs decorate aspic shell for Ham and Tongue Aspic (Recipe 239). Eggs are dipped in aspic, then attached to sides of mould.

23a. Melon mould with cherries (Recipe 219), turned out on a bed of fresh mint, is garnished with cantaloup balls. Fruits used in the moulded salad are cantaloup, cherries, and pineapple. Cherry juice colours the jelly base deep purple, and pineapple juice gives it added flavour.

23b. To make melon mould shown above and described (in Recipe 219), first dissolve jelly in hot pineapple juice. Add cherry juice. Chill. Peel cantaloup, cut into cubes, and place in bottom of mould. Add pineapple and cherries to chilled jelly and pour over cantaloup cubes.

24a. Avocado and Tomato Salad (Recipe 217) looks festive when you mould it in a fluted mould and garnish it with cherry tomatoes, lemon wedges, and avocado slices. To make it, you mould an avocado-sour cream aspic on top of a tomato aspic. Serve it with sliced smoked salmon for a summer luncheon.

24b. Orange, pineapple, and apricot layers form this eye-catching salad (Recipe 227). Salted almonds fill the centre of the ring and prunes stuffed with mandarin oranges surround it.

Meat, Poultry, and Seafood Salads

Meat, Fish, and Poultry

Meat, fish, and poultry salads are the hearty members of the salad family. They are usually served as main courses at luncheon or supper, but in small servings many of them are suitable for a first course or as part of an *hors d'œuvre*.

You will find some famous salads in this group. The Crab Louis has become a classic salad in the United States, and the dressing used for it is now incorporated in other fish salads as well. The Cobb salad is another old favourite abroad, and you will find prawns are delicious dressed with a version of the famous Green Goddess salad dressing.

Salads in this chapter can often be made of leftovers. Chunky bits of leftover chicken, for example, make an ideal salad for a party luncheon when they are combined with orange-coloured apricot slices, bits of spring onion, and crisp water chestnuts. Creamy cottage cheese and crunchy celery stretch leftover ham into a main course salad.

Most of the salads that follow here have one thing in common. They make use of crisp ingredients, such as green pepper, cucumber, pickles, nuts, celery, water chestnuts, to offset the smoother, heavier textures of meat, fish and poultry.

148. Beef or Veal Salad

2 tablespoons tomato paste
¼ teaspoon prepared horseradish
3 tablespoons vinegar
2 tablespoons meat stock or
    fat-free meat juices
1 lb. thinly sliced lean beef or
    veal (from roast or broiled
    steak cooked rare)
Salt and pepper
Salad greens (part watercress,
    if desired)
Radishes

Here's a hearty meat salad enriched by an almost-no-calorie dressing.

Blend together tomato paste, horseradish, vinegar, and meat stock. Toss with meat. Season to taste with salt and pepper. Let chill at least 1 hour. Serve on a bed of mixed salad greens and garnish with decoratively cut radishes. Makes 4 to 6 servings.

149. Veal and Bacon Salad

6 medium-sized tomatoes
1 teaspoon salt
6 lettuce cups
1½ lb. diced, cooked veal
¼ cup sliced celery
¼ cup crumbled, crisp bacon
¼ cup sliced radishes
1½ gills mayonnaise

Cold leftover veal can be used in this hearty salad. The cubed meat, crisp vegetables, and bacon are spooned into sectioned tomato cups.

Peel tomatoes and cut in 6 sections – but not all the way through – so they will open like a flower. Sprinkle with salt. Arrange in lettuce cups. Chill. Toss together the veal, celery, bacon, and radishes. Mix in the mayonnaise. Spoon salad into tomato shells. Makes 6 servings.

150. Ham Slaw

¼ pint soured cream
2 tablespoons mayonnaise
2–4 tablespoons crumbled
*   blue cheese*
2 tablespoons finely chopped
*   green pepper or spring onion*
1 saltspoon salt
1 tablespoon wine vinegar
4 cups finely shredded cabbage
1 thinly sliced large apple
½–1 lb. cold boiled ham,
*   cut in cubes or thin strips*

Blue cheese flavours this hearty cabbage and ham salad, a good choice for a luncheon.

Blend soured cream, mayonnaise, cheese, green pepper or onion, salt, and vinegar. Chill several hours. In a large salad bowl, put cabbage, apple, and ham. Pour dressing over salad and toss gently. Makes 6 to 8 servings.

151. Ham–Vegetable–Cottage Cheese Salad

¼ cup diced or slivered boiled
  ham
¼ cup sliced celery
¾ cup boiled peas
¾ cup stoned olives, sliced
8 oz. cottage cheese
2 tablespoons mayonnaise
¼ teaspoon salt
Salad greens
Paprika to taste

In this main-course salad, you get a wide range of colours as well as of
flavours. The creamy cottage cheese provides a smooth background for
the crunch of celery.

Mix together the ham, celery, peas, and sliced olives. Combine the cottage cheese, mayonnaise, and salt, and toss together with the ham and
vegetable salad mixture. Heap in a salad bowl lined with greens or spoon
into lettuce cups for individual salads. Sprinkle the top with paprika.
Makes 4 generous servings.

152. Ham and Sausage Salad Bowl

1 tin (2¼ oz.) devilled ham
4 oz. Frankfurter or Vienna
  sausages
1 medium-sized lettuce
1 bunch watercress
1 small bunch radishes
1 cucumber
4 spring onions
¼ pint French dressing (not too
  salty)

Devilled ham and Frankfurter or Vienna sausages are spicy accents in
this salad that is almost a meal in itself.

Chill ham and sausages well. Cut ham in small cubes, and slice sausages
in ½-inch lengths. Break the lettuce and watercress into small pieces and
place in a salad bowl. Slice radishes, cucumber, and onions. Arrange on
top of lettuce, along with devilled ham and sliced sausages. Pour French
dressing over and toss. Makes 6 servings.

153. Supper Salad

1½ cups diced cooked ham,
   pork, veal, or turkey
¼ cup diced boiled potatoes
¼ cup each cooked peas and
   green lima beans
¼ cup cooked green beans, cut
   in 1-inch lengths

½ cup sliced cooked carrots
¼ pint French dressing
¼ cup chopped sweet pickle
2 hard-boiled eggs, chopped
1½ gills mayonnaise
Salt, pepper, and paprika
Crisp salad greens

Here's the 'build-up' technique – meat, eggs, potatoes, and colourful
cooked vegetables.

Place the ham, potatoes, carrots, peas, lima beans, and green beans in a
salad bowl. Pour French dressing over, toss lightly, and chill for at least
1 hour. When you are ready to serve, add the pickle, eggs, and mayonnaise. Mix lightly. Season to taste with salt, pepper, and paprika. Serve
on crisp greens. Makes 6 servings.

154. Buffet Salad Bowl

1 medium-sized lettuce
2 large tomatoes, quartered
2 hard-boiled eggs, halved
1 cup cubed luncheon meat
¼ cup American cheese, cut in
   strips
6 spring onions, chopped
Burgundy Dressing

Shred lettuce coarsely. Arrange in salad bowl with tomatoes, eggs, meat,
and cheese on top. Sprinkle with the chopped onion. Before serving, toss
all ingredients together with Burgundy Dressing. Makes 4 or 5 servings.

BURGUNDY DRESSING:

1 teaspoon salt
1 teaspoon sugar
¼ teaspoon dry mustard
Dash of pepper

2 tablespoons grated onion
¼ pint Burgundy
½ gill cider vinegar
½ gill salad oil

Measure ingredients in the order given into a screw-top jar. Cover and
shake until well blended. Makes about ½ pint dressing.

155. Frankfurter Club Salad

6 Frankfurters
2 firm tomatoes
2 cups cooked lima beans
1 cup Swiss, jack, or Cheddar
  cheese cubes
Club Salad Dressing
6 strips crisply fried bacon
2–3 cups torn crisp lettuce

Cut Frankfurters in ½-inch diagonal slices. Cut tomatoes into eighths.
Arrange Frankfurters, tomatoes, limas, and cheese in separate piles in
a large salad bowl. Pour over half the dressing. Marinate in refrigerator
for several hours. When ready to serve, coarsely crumble bacon into
bowl, add lettuce, and toss with additional dressing until ingredients are
well coated. Makes 6 to 8 servings.

CLUB SALAD DRESSING:
¼ pint salad oil
4 tablespoons wine vinegar
1 small clove garlic
  minced or mashed

3 spring onions, chopped
¼ teaspoon paprika
½ teaspoon dry mustard
¾ teaspoon salt
¼ teaspoon dill seed

Shake all ingredients together in a covered jar until blended. Makes
½ pint.

156. Sweetbread Salad with Grapes

Wash 3 lb. of sweetbreads and cook in acidulated water (add juice of ½
lemon and 1 teaspoon salt to each quart) for 20 minutes. Drain and
plunge them into cold water. When cold remove membrane and dark
spots, and cut in pieces the size of grapes. Cover with ¼ pint French
dressing and chill. When ready to serve, combine with 1 lb. seedless (or
halved and seeded) grapes, 2 cups minced celery, and ¾ pint mayonnaise.
Mix gently. Add salt and more mayonnaise if necessary. Chill, and
serve from a large bowl. Makes about 12 servings.

157. Hot Frankfurter Salad

5 or 6 large hot boiled
    potatoes
2 stalks celery
5 radishes
6 slices crisply fried bacon

1 medium-sized lettuce
1 cup boiled peas
Frankfurter Dressing
3 hard-boiled eggs, sliced
Crisp lettuce leaves

Reminiscent of German hot potato salad, this main-course salad has a
delicious sweet–sour dressing.

Peel and cube potatoes. Slice celery and radishes, and break bacon into
large pieces. Tear lettuce into bite-size pieces. Toss all together gently
with peas and dressing. Heap back into the warm pan. Garnish top with
eggs and around edge with lettuce leaves. Makes 6 to 8 servings.

FRANKFURTER DRESSING:
Boiling water
6 Frankfurters
1 small onion, finely chopped
¼ gill bacon drippings
2 tablespoons flour

½ pint chicken stock
4 tablespoons vinegar
1 teaspoon salt
Few grains pepper
1 teaspoon celery seed
½ tablespoon caster sugar

Pour boiling water over Frankfurters and let stand 5 minutes. Sauté
onion in bacon drippings until soft but not browned. Blend in flour.
Add stock slowly. Cook and stir until smooth and thickened. Stir in
vinegar, salt, pepper, celery seed, and sugar. Cook 5 minutes more.
Drain the Frankfurters, slice, and add to dressing.

158. Corned Beef–Potato Salad

1½ cups diced boiled potatoes
¼ cup finely sliced celery and
    leaves
¼ cup chopped sweet pickle
1 teaspoon grated onion
6 oz. cubed corned beef

¼ pint mayonnaise or salad
    dressing
1 teaspoon prepared mustard
3 tablespoons chilli sauce
¼ teaspoon salt
Dash of pepper

In this hearty salad, a well-seasoned, spicy dressing binds cubed corned
beef and potatoes together.

Combine potatoes, celery, pickle, onion, and corned beef. Blend mayonnaise, mustard, chilli sauce, salt, and pepper. Pour over potato mixture
and toss lightly. Chill thoroughly. Garnish, if desired, with crisp lettuce
leaves, tomato wedges, and carrot curls. Makes 4 servings.

159. Hearty Chef's Salad

¼ pint French dressing
1 cup boiled, stringless beans
1 cup 2-inch carrot sticks,
* cooked*
1 cup 2-inch raw celery sticks
1 medium-sized lettuce
1 cup cooked ham slivers, cut
* ¼ inch thick*
½ cup Swiss cheese strips, cut
* ¼ inch thick*
2 hard-boiled eggs, sliced
1½ gills mayonnaise
2–3 tablespoons chilli sauce
1 tablespoon grated horseradish

Pour French dressing over green beans, carrot sticks, and celery sticks.
Toss lightly and chill for 2 hours. Drain. Tear lettuce into eight pieces
and arrange around the edge of a large salad bowl. Pile drained vegetables, ham slivers, and cheese strips in the centre of the bowl. Arrange
egg slices around the vegetable mixture. Beat together until smooth the
mayonnaise, chilli sauce, and horseradish. Spoon over salad and serve
immediately. Makes 8 servings.

160. Salade de Maison

3 firm tomatoes
1 whole cooked chicken breast
3 anchovy fillets
2 hard-boiled eggs
1 bunch watercress
1 head crisp lettuce
French dressing
Curry powder

Peel tomatoes, discard juice and seeds, and chop the pulp. Remove skin
from chicken and cut the meat in small cubes. Chop the anchovy fillets,
eggs, and watercress. Cut the lettuce in small chunks. Combine the
tomatoes, chicken, anchovy fillets, eggs, watercress, and lettuce in a large
bowl. Pour over enough French dressing – seasoned with curry powder
to taste – to moisten salad, and toss. Makes 6 servings.

161. Chicken Salad Piquant

2 large whole chicken breasts
  (about 1 lb.)
½ pint water
1 teaspoon salt
2 tablespoons white wine
  vinegar
1 teaspoon grated orange peel

2 spring onions, thinly sliced
  (including part of the tops)
2 large oranges, peeled and
  thinly sliced
Salt and pepper
Salad greens

The dressing for this delicious chicken and orange salad has only about
2 calories per tablespoon.

In a small saucepan, combine chicken, water, and salt. Bring to the boil.
Cover and simmer slowly 15 to 20 minutes, or until chicken is tender. Let
cool in stock. Strain and save stock. Discard skin and bones and cut
meat in thin strips or thin slices. Mix together ¼ pint chicken stock,
vinegar, orange peel, and onions. Pour this dressing over chicken. Add
oranges. Chill 1 hour. Season with salt and pepper. Serve on salad greens.
Makes 4 to 6 servings.

162. Apricot Chicken Salad

¾–1 lb. diced cooked chicken
¾ lb. sliced fresh apricots
1 cup thinly sliced water
  chestnuts or celery
1 tablespoon finely chopped
  onion
3 tablespoons soured cream
3 tablespoons mayonnaise
1½ tablespoons lemon juice
Salt to taste
4 or 5 lettuce cups

Bits of green onion and orange apricot slices among chunks of chicken
make this salad pretty enough for a special luncheon. For a different way
to serve it, you might heap the salad on a bed of crisp chow mein noodles
rather than into lettuce cups.

Toss together lightly the chicken, apricots, water chestnuts, onion,
soured cream, mayonnaise, lemon juice, and salt. Serve in crisp lettuce
cups. Makes 4 or 5 servings.

163. Chicken Breast Salad

6 whole, boned chicken breasts
3 oz. cream cheese
¼ cup mayonnaise
2 teaspoons lemon juice
¼ teaspoon grated lemon peel
Dash of salt
1 finely chopped spring onion
    and top

Crisp lettuce
2 or 3 large tomatoes, peeled
    and chilled
Salt and pepper
2 large avocados
½ cup toasted slivered almonds
    (optional)
Stoned ripe olives

Cook chicken breasts until tender (you can either fry them in butter, covered to keep them moist, or simmer them in stock). Chill breasts. Remove skin and pat dry. Mix together thoroughly the cream cheese, mayonnaise, lemon juice, lemon peel, salt, and onion.

Coat rounded side of each piece of chicken completely with cheese dressing. Arrange crisp lettuce on 6 dinner-size plates. Cut tomatoes into 6 thick slices and place on lettuce. Sprinkle with salt and pepper. Arrange a coated chicken breast on each tomato slice. Halve and peel avocados, and cut each half into 3 slices. Place 2 avocado slices on each plate. Sprinkle chicken with toasted almonds and garnish with ripe olives. Makes 6 servings.

164. Chicken-Curry Salad

4 to 5 cups cooked chicken or
    turkey, in large chunks
2 teaspoons grated onion
1 cup celery, cut in diagonal
    slices
1 cup finely chopped green pepper
½ gill light cream

About ¼ pint mayonnaise or
    salad dressing
1 teaspoon salt
1 saltspoon pepper
1 teaspoon curry powder
2 tablespoons vinegar
Crisp salad greens

To heighten the delicate curry flavour, let this salad blend for several hours in the refrigerator.

Combine the chicken with onion, celery, and pepper. For the dressing, mix cream with mayonnaise, salt, pepper, curry, and vinegar. Add dressing to the chicken and toss lightly. Refrigerate until time to serve. Arrange the salad in a serving bowl or on individual plates. Surround with crisp salad greens. Makes 6 to 8 servings.

165. Chilean Corn and Chicken Salad

2 ears of cooked corn   ½ pint mayonnaise
1 cup diced cooked chicken   ½ teaspoon chilli powder
1½ cups chopped peeled tomatoes Salt and pepper
1 green pepper, seeded and   Lettuce leaves and stuffed green
   chopped   olives for garnish

Cooked corn is good in salads. Run the knife close to the cob so you don't split the corn kernels.

With a sharp knife, cut the cooked corn kernels from the cob. Mix together the corn, chicken, tomatoes, green pepper, mayonnaise, and chilli powder. Season with salt and pepper to taste. Chill. To serve, arrange on a platter or individual salad plates lined with lettuce leaves. Spoon corn mixture into the centre or centres. Garnish with olives. Makes 4 to 6 servings.

166. Duck and Orange Mayonnaise

¾ pint chopped cooked duck
French dressing as required
Celery salt to taste
1 tablespoon chopped cashew nuts
¼ pint chopped seedless orange
1½ gills boiled green peas
Mayonnaise as required
Parsley and mint as required
Curly endive as required

Sprinkle duck with French dressing. Cover and stand for 2 hours. Drain well. Add celery salt, nuts, orange, green peas, and mayonnaise to coat, about 4 or 5 tablespoons. Season if necessary with salt and pepper. Divide equally among 4 individual salad plates. Place a sprig of parsley in the centre of each portion. Sprinkle chopped mint round. Fringe with one or two sprigs of curly endive, coated with French dressing. Serve with additional mayonnaise in a bowl. Makes 4 servings.

NOTE: When required for a party, halve 8 large oranges. Carefully scoop out the flesh and all membrane. Vandyke round the edges with scissors. Fill oranges with salad. Place each on an individual plate, and arrange the endive round the base. Garnish with parsley and mint as described. (For 8 servings increase amount of duck to 1¼ pints.)

167. Crunchy Chicken Salad

¼ pint mayonnaise
1½ teaspoons prepared mustard
About 2 tablespoons sweet
  pickle juice
Salt and freshly ground black
  pepper to taste
6 cups cooked chicken cut in
  chunks
4 cups sliced celery (including
  a few tender leaves)
1 large cucumber, diced

3 tablespoons chopped green
  pepper
3 tablespoons grated mild
  onion
8 sweet pickles, diced
Coarsely shredded lettuce
Large, stoned ripe olives
2 large firm tomatoes, sliced
4 hard-boiled eggs, sliced
Paprika

This chicken salad is full of crunchy celery, cucumbers, and pickles, as
well as big chunks of chicken. It is well worth trying.

Mix mayonnaise and mustard. Add enough pickle juice to thin to a desired consistency. Add salt and pepper. Pour dressing over chicken,
celery, green pepper, onion, cucumber, and pickles in a large mixing
bowl. Toss lightly.
  At serving time, turn salad into a large salad bowl lined with shredded
lettuce. Garnish with olives, tomato slices, and egg slices. Sprinkle the
egg slices with paprika. Makes 12 servings.

168. Cauliflower Chicken Salad

1 cup chopped cooked chicken
1 small head (3 cups) finely
  chopped raw cauliflower
3 tablespoons sliced pimiento-
  stuffed green olives
3 tablespoons finely chopped
  parsley

3 tablespoons chilli sauce
2 tablespoons mayonnaise
1 tablespoon vinegar
2 teaspoons olive oil
1 teaspoon salt
¼ teaspoon pepper
6–8 lettuce cups

Fresh crisp cauliflower serves as a base for this colourful chicken salad.
Serve individually in lettuce cups with a garnish of mayonnaise and a
dash of paprika.
Combine chicken, cauliflower, olives, and parsley in large bowl. Mix
thoroughly. Blend together chilli sauce, mayonnaise, vinegar, olive oil,
salt, and pepper. Stir into salad, and toss thoroughly. Chill. Serve in
lettuce cups. Makes 6 to 8 servings.

169. Chicken Salad with Roquefort Dressing

4 whole, cooked chicken breasts
1 cup sliced celery
2 tablespoons finely sliced
   spring onions
1 tablespoon each mustard and
   lemon juice
¼ teaspoon salt
Freshly ground pepper to taste

Dash of cayenne
Roquefort dressing
4 rashers bacon
4 cups torn cos lettuce leaves
Lemon wedges, sliced stuffed
   olives, and parsley sprigs for
   garnish

Carve chicken from bone, then cut into good-sized chunks. Toss with
celery, onions, mustard, lemon juice, salt, pepper, cayenne, and enough
Roquefort dressing to moisten (about ¼ pint). Chill thoroughly. Cook
bacon until very crisp. Drain, crumble, and set aside. Toss lettuce leaves
with Roquefort dressing to coat. Arrange lettuce leaves in bottom of 4
chilled salad bowls. Top each with a mound of chicken salad. Sprinkle
with crumbled bacon. Garnish with lemon wedges, sliced stuffed olives,
and parsley sprigs. Makes 4 servings.

170. Turkey Salad in
Pineapple Shells

6 cups cubed cooked turkey
¾ lb. coarsely chopped
   walnuts
2 cups sliced celery
1 teaspoon salt
1¼–1½ pints mayonnaise
1 large pineapple

A scooped-out pineapple shell makes a festive bowl for this turkey-and-
nut salad.

Mix together the turkey, nuts, celery, salt, and mayonnaise. Cut the
pineapple in half lengthwise and remove fruit from shells. (To keep the
salad cold on the table, freeze the shells before filling with the salad.)
Fill the pineapple half shells with turkey salad and arrange on a large
platter. Garnish with a few pieces of the fresh pineapple. Makes 12
servings.

171. Chicken Salad with Avocado and Greens

¾ pint mayonnaise
6 oz. seedless raisins
4 oz. salted peanuts
½ pint mango chutney, cut into
  slivers
4 oz. flaked coconut
2 lb. cooked chicken meat,
  diced coarsely

2 cups diagonally sliced ripe
  bananas
Salt and pepper to taste
Salad greens
Additional sliced bananas
Avocado slices
Lemon juice

This unusual chicken salad is so delicious you'll probably want to serve
it on special occasions, perhaps as the entrée for a buffet salad luncheon.
To plump the raisins, let them stand in white wine a few hours before
making the salad. Drain thoroughly before using.

Mix together the mayonnaise, raisins, peanuts, chutney, and coconut.
Toss with chicken meat. Gently combine with sliced bananas. Season
with salt and pepper. Mound in a large lettuce bowl or on a platter
lined with shredded lettuce and lettuce leaves. Garnish with slices of
avocado and banana, which you have dipped into lemon juice. Makes
12 servings.

172. Cobb Salad

1 large lettuce
1 bunch watercress
3 hard-boiled eggs
12 rashers crisply fried bacon,
  crumbled
4 tablespoons crumbled
  Roquefort or blue cheese

4 medium-sized tomatoes, peeled
2 medium-sized avocados
2 boned cooked chicken breasts
1 tablespoon chopped chives
Crisp lettuce
French dressing

Using the large blade of your mincer or a French knife or cutting tool,
coarsely chop the lettuce, watercress leaves (omit stems), eggs, bacon,
cheese, tomatoes, avocados, chicken, and chives. Line plates with crisp
lettuce and pile salad on the plates, peaking it up. Garnish with olives,
radishes, and avocado slices, if desired. Hand the dressing separately.
Makes 4 servings.

173. Nun's Salad

Here is a good way to use up bits of cold turkey. Combine 3 cups cold boiled rice with enough mustard-flavoured French dressing to moisten well, then gently fold in 1 cup (or more) of cold turkey cut in julienne pieces. Heap in a lettuce-lined bowl and sprinkle the top with minced ripe olives. Makes 4 to 6 servings.

174. Exotic Luncheon Salad

Coarsely cut cooked turkey
1 large tin (20 oz.) water
  chestnuts
2 lb. seedless grapes
2 cups sliced celery
10–15 oz. toasted slivered
  almonds
1¼ pints mayonnaise
1 tablespoon curry powder
1–2 tablespoons soy sauce
Crisp lettuce
1 large tin (20 oz.) litchi nuts or
  1 large tin (1 lb. 13 oz.)
  pineapple chunks

This salad is elegance itself. Chunks of pineapple can be used in place of the litchi nuts.

Use turkey breast meat. (You will need 2½ to 3 lb.) Coarsely cut the turkey meat from bone into bite-size pieces.

Slice or dice the water chestnuts, and mix them with the turkey meat. Wash the grapes. Pick them from their stems, and add, along with the celery and 7–10 oz. of the toasted almonds. Mix the mayonnaise with the curry powder and soy sauce. (You may like a couple of tablespoons of lemon juice with it, too.) Combine with the turkey mixture. Chill for several hours, then spoon into nests of lettuce. Sprinkle with the remaining toasted almonds and garnish with the litchi nuts or pineapple chunks arranged on top of each serving. This recipe makes 12 generous servings. It can be easily multiplied to serve a larger party.

175. Fruited Turkey Salad

6–8 large slices cooked turkey
1½ cups cubed cooked turkey
1 cup chopped apple or celery
3 oz. seeded grapes or tinned
  seedless grapes, drained
¼ cup pineapple chunks, fresh
  or frozen
3 tablespoons pomegranate seeds

3 tablespoons soured cream
¼ cup mayonnaise
1 tablespoon lemon juice
½ teaspoon grated lemon peel
1 teaspoon grated onion
½ teaspoon salt
Few grains cayenne pepper
Watercress or shredded lettuce

This salad is a mixture of fresh fruit and turkey, served in individual cornucopias formed with turkey slices – or with ham slices, if you prefer.

To make the cornucopias, roll the turkey slices into cone shapes. Fasten the narrow ends with a cocktail stick. For the filling toss together cubed turkey, apple (or celery), grapes, pineapple, and pomegranate seeds. Blend remaining ingredients. Add to fruit mixture. Toss lightly. Makes enough filling for 6 to 8 cornucopias. Garnish salad platter with watercress or shredded lettuce.

176. Crawfish Salad

1 tin (5¼ oz.) cubed crawfish
  tails
1 cup thinly sliced celery
3 tablespoons chopped spring
  onions, including some of
  the tops
6 radishes, thinly sliced crosswise

¼ cup diced green pepper
2 tablespoons chopped
  pimiento
7 or 8 green olives, chopped
Mayonnaise (about ¼ pint)
6 lettuce cups
Hard-boiled eggs

This salad contains chunks of richly flavoured canned crawfish tails, tossed with a combination of red and green vegetables, and mounded in crisp lettuce cups. It would make an unusual first course for a party meal.

Toss together crawfish cubes, celery, onion, radishes, green pepper, pimiento, and green olives with mayonnaise to moisten. Arrange lettuce cups on a platter, or individual serving dishes, and fill with salad. Garnish with egg slices. Makes 6 servings.

177. Crab Louis

½ pint mayonnaise
¼ gill whipping cream
3 tablespoons chilli sauce
*3 tablespoons chopped green
  pepper*
*3 tablespoons chopped spring
  onion*
Salt to taste
Lemon juice to taste
2 crisp lettuces
*2 large crabs, cracked and
  shelled, or 1½–2 lb. crab meat*
4 large tomatoes
4 hard-boiled eggs

Which Louis originated this hearty, full-meal salad, we do not know, but
Solari's Grill in San Francisco was among the first restaurants to serve
it, around 1911. Now it is a favourite in many restaurants. The Louis
dressing is good on shrimp, too.

Mix together the mayonnaise, whipping cream, chilli sauce, green
pepper, and green onion. Season with salt and lemon juice to taste.
Arrange outer leaves of lettuce on 4 large plates. Shred the heart of the
lettuce and arrange a bed of shredded lettuce in the centre of the leaves.
Place the body meat of the crabs on the shredded lettuce. Cut tomatoes
and eggs in sixths and arrange symmetrically around the crab. Pour the
Louis dressing over, and garnish with crab legs. Makes 4 servings.

178. Crab and Artichoke Salad
with Sour Cream Dressing

Place a thick wedge of chilled crisp lettuce on 8 individual salad plates.
Blend together ½ pint soured cream, 2 tablespoons minced chives, and the
juice of 1 lemon. Cut in small pieces 1 jar or tin (about 6 oz.) pickled
artichoke hearts. Add to sour cream mixture with liquid from jar or tin.
Season to taste with salt. Spoon an equal amount on each serving of
lettuce. Garnish each with 1 or 2 crab legs, blend 1 cup flaked crab meat
with dressing and use instead. Makes 8 servings.

179. Coconut Crab Salad

1 medium-sized grapefruit
1 medium-sized avocado
4 cooked artichoke hearts
1 small lettuce, shredded
2 oz. flaked coconut
1 lb. crab meat
¼ pint mayonnaise
*2 tablespoons dry white table
    wine*
3 tablespoons lemon juice
¼ teaspoon salt
Pepper to taste
Lettuce

Peel grapefruit and lift segments out of membrane into salad bowl, re-serving a few for the garnish. Peel avocado, and slice. Set aside a few slices and sprinkle with lemon juice. Add remaining grapefruit and avocado to bowl, then 2 of the artichoke hearts sliced, saving 2 for garnish. Add shredded lettuce, coconut, and crab meat. Mix together dressing of mayonnaise, wine, lemon juice, salt, and pepper. Pour about half over ingredients in salad bowl. Toss lightly. Heap salad into 6 lettuce-lined bowls. Garnish with remaining grapefruit sections, avocado slices, and artichoke slices. Pass remaining salad dressing in a small bowl. Makes 6 servings.

180. Pineapple with Crab Salad

Cut the fruit from 1 pineapple into 6 slices. Cut out the cores. On each of 6 salad plates, arrange crisp watercress or small tender spinach leaves. Set a pineapple slice on each, then arrange 4 or 5 crab legs on each slice of pineapple (you'll need ¾–1 pound fresh, frozen, or tinned crab). Serve with the following dressing. Makes 6 servings.

ROSY LIME DRESSING:
Combine ¼ pint tomato ketchup with ½ gill fresh lime juice (or you may prefer lemon juice). Blend until smooth.

181. Oyster Salad

½ pint tarragon vinegar
1½ pints water
1 teaspoon salt
1 teaspoon tarragon
2 pints oysters
½ pint mayonnaise
1 teaspoon lemon juice

1 tablespoon anchovy paste
1 teaspoon grated onion
Salt and white pepper to taste
1 large bunch celery
Anchovy fillets and stuffed
   green olives

If you serve generous portions of this salad, it makes an ideal main dish
for a luncheon. It can also accompany baked ham or tongue, perhaps at
a guest buffet.

Combine tarragon vinegar with water, salt, and tarragon. Bring to the
boil. Add oysters and cook for about 2 minutes, or just until the oysters
plump and begin to curl on the edges. Drain oysters and chill thoroughly.
Mix mayonnaise with lemon juice, anchovy paste, and onion. To serve,
mix half of mayonnaise mixture with the oysters. Season with salt and
pepper. Slice celery very finely and make a bed of it on a platter or individual plates. Mound oysters on top. Top with remaining mayonnaise
mixture, and garnish with anchovy fillets and olives. Makes 4 main-
course servings or about 8 smaller servings.

182. Oyster and Tomato Salad

½ pint water
1 tablespoon vinegar
½ teaspoon salt
Freshly ground pepper
1 pint medium-sized oysters
6 thick tomato slices
Lettuce
½ pint mayonnaise
2 teaspoons anchovy paste
1 teaspoon lemon juice

Heat the water, vinegar, salt, and a dash of freshly ground pepper to
boiling point. Add oysters. Poach gently for about 3 minutes. Chill, and
drain. For each serving, place a slice of tomato on lettuce. Top with
oysters. Serve with anchovy mayonnaise made by blending the mayonnaise, anchovy paste, and lemon juice. Makes 6 servings.

187. Shrimp and Bean Sprout Salad

1 lb. fresh bean sprouts
*2 spring onions (including
    tops), minced*
*½ pint cooked prawns, shrimps, or
    crab meat*
½ pint yogurt
1 teaspoon curry powder
Pressed garlic
1 or 2 tablespoons lemon juice
2 tablespoons soy sauce
Sugar, if desired

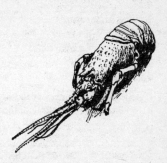

In the Orient, preparation of bean sprouts always includes removing the hair-like root. If you're short of time, however, this is not really necessary.

Prepare bean sprouts by pinching off and discarding the hair-like root. Combine with onions and fish. Toss with yogurt mixed with curry, a little garlic, lemon juice, soy sauce, and sugar to taste. Makes 4 to 6 servings.

188. Shrimp and Rice Salad

2 oz. uncooked white rice or
6 oz. boiled rice
½ pint boiled shrimps
¾ teaspoon salt
*1 tablespoon chopped stuffed
    green olives*
*3 tablespoons slivered green
    pepper*

¾ cup chopped raw cauliflower
3 tablespoons lemon juice
2 tablespoons French dressing
4 tablespoons mayonnaise
1 tablespoon chopped onion
Pepper to taste
4 lettuce cups

Shrimps, rice, and green pepper team well together. Here they are chilled and made into a salad, and their textures and flavours are equally pleasing.

Cook rice according to any preferred method until tender. Cool. Toss the cooked rice, shrimps, salt, cauliflower, stuffed green olives, and green pepper lightly together. Blend the lemon juice with the French dressing, mayonnaise, onion, and pepper to taste. Pour dressing over salad and toss. Spoon into lettuce cups. Makes 4 servings.

189. Shrimp-stuffed Artichokes

8 large globe artichokes
Boiling salted water
Tart French dressing
4 tablespoons mayonnaise
1 tablespoon lemon juice
¾ pint shelled shrimps

4 tablespoons stoned ripe
  olives, sliced
1½ cups diced celery
Salt
Pepper
Paprika

Overflowing the centres of these artichokes is a colourful shrimp salad.
If you like artichokes chilled, these should suit your fancy.

Wash artichokes. Cut off tips and stem ends, and pull off tough outer
leaves. In a covered saucepan, steam artichokes in 2 inches of boiling
salted water for 35 to 45 minutes, or until tender. Drain. Turn artichokes
upside down to cool. Gently spread the outer leaves to form a cup, and
using a teaspoon, scoop out the choke. Cover each artichoke with French
dressing, and chill.
    When ready to serve, combine mayonnaise and lemon juice, and toss
lightly with shrimps, olives, and celery. Heap into drained artichoke cups,
and sprinkle with salt, pepper, and paprika. Serve chilled. Makes 8
servings.

190. Shrimp Vegetable Salad

1 peeled clove garlic
2 oz. butter
4 slices day-old bread
1 package (10 oz.) frozen peas
  cooked and chilled
¼ pint shelled shrimps
3–4 tablespoons mayonnaise

1 tablespoon light cream
1 tablespoon lemon juice
2 whole spring onions, finely sliced
2 pinches sweet basil
Salt
Shredded lettuce

The most interesting part of this recipe is the unusual texture contrast
of shrimps, tender peas, and crunchy garlic croûtons.

Rub a bowl well with a cut clove of garlic. Then mash or mince remaining garlic and mix with melted butter in a small frying pan. Remove
bread crusts and cut bread in small ½-inch cubes. Brown cubes in the
garlic butter over a low heat, tossing until light brown and all the butter
has been absorbed. Cool. Combine peas, shrimps, mayonnaise, cream,
lemon juice, onions and tops, and sweet basil. Salt to taste. Stir in garlic
croûtons just before serving. Serve on shredded lettuce. Makes 4 servings.

191. Curried Shrimp

Shell, clean, and cook 1½ pints shrimps in court bouillon. Combine with dressing (½ pint mayonnaise, ¼ pint chilli sauce, 1 tablespoon curry powder, 1 to 2 tablespoons lemon juice). Serve on individual plates lined with endive, chicory, or cos lettuce, and sprinkle with chopped salted almonds. Makes 6 servings.

192. Prawn Salad with Green Goddess Dressing

2 lb. large uncooked prawns
1 quart celery pieces
Green Goddess Dressing
Parsley

The night before, shell and de-vein prawns. Put prawns in a large saucepan, cover with water, and bring to the boil. Remove immediately from heat. Allow to cool for 15 minutes. Rinse in cold water and cut each prawn in half lengthwise (save a few whole ones for garnish). Pick whitest stalks of celery. Clean thoroughly. Cut in ⅛-inch-thick slices. Combine with prawns and refrigerate overnight. Dress with Green Goddess Dressing to barely coat (about ½ pint). Pile lightly into a shallow salad bowl lined with large leaves of crisp lettuce. Garnish with whole prawns and parsley sprigs. Serve additional dressing on the side. Makes 16 servings.

GREEN GODDESS DRESSING:
1 pint mayonnaise
¼ pint white wine vinegar
1 small tin (2 oz.) rolled
  anchovies with capers
¼ cup chopped fresh parsley
1 small onion, finely chopped
  (about ¼ pint)
2 teaspoons dried tarragon leaves
¼ teaspoon salt
¼ pint whipping cream

Place mayonnaise, 1½ gills of the vinegar, drained anchovies, parsley, onion, tarragon, and salt into a blender. Whirl until thoroughly blended. Combine remaining vinegar with cream and add to first mixture. Whirl again. Store in refrigerator until needed. Makes 2 pints dressing.

193. Prawns with Lemon Dressing

The tinned prawns on this platter regain their fresh-caught flavour with
an ice-cube chilling and a few hours' marinating in a lemony dressing.
Drain 1 tin (4½ oz.) prawns. Rinse in cold water. Chill in bowl of ice
cubes and water 15 minutes; drain. Add to dressing made of 2 tablespoons tart French dressing, 1 tablespoon lemon juice, 1 teaspoon soy
sauce, and 3 drops Tabasco. Chill. Mix prawns and dressing with 4 tablespoons finely sliced celery. Serve on crisp watercress. Makes 1 serving
as a main-course salad.

194. Salmon and Shrimp Salad

¾ lb. chilled flaked, boiled, or
    steamed salmon
¼ pint chilled shelled shrimps
¾ pint diced drained cucumber
1 teaspoon minced onion or
    shallot
Salt and pepper to taste

Mayonnaise as required
2 hearts of lettuce
French dressing as required
Thin slices of beetroot as
    required
1 tablespoon chopped capers
Paprika to taste

Place salmon and shrimps in a basin. Drain cucumber on a cloth for 15
minutes. Add to fish. Sprinkle with onion or shallot. Season to taste
with salt and pepper. Add mayonnaise to coat. Toss fish with the mayonnaise. Soak lettuce in French dressing to moisten for 2 or 3 minutes,
then quarter. Arrange quartered hearts around a salad bowl. Place salmon
mixture in centre. Garnish with beetroot, capers, and paprika, and a
little mustard and cress if liked. Makes 4 or 5 servings.

195. Tuna Salad Niçoise

A tuna salad that makes a fine luncheon dish or first course at dinner is
called Niçoise because it originated in Nice.

Slice 1 head of lettuce and arrange it in a large shallow bowl. On it,
in a symmetrical design, arrange 4 small peeled and quartered tomatoes,
1 cup cooked green beans, 1 cup diced, boiled potatoes, 1 onion, sliced
thinly and the slices halved, 2 sliced hard-boiled eggs, and 1 tin (7 oz.)
tuna. Garnish with 6–8 anchovy fillets and some black olives. Just before
serving, pour French dressing over. Makes 6 to 8 servings.

196. Tuna, Banana, Pineapple Salad

3 ripe bananas
1 cup drained diced pineapple
¼ cup sliced celery
¼ teaspoon salt
1¼ gills salad dressing
2 tablespoons lemon juice
1 tin (7 oz.) tuna, flaked
Lettuce

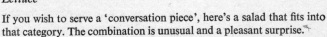

If you wish to serve a 'conversation piece', here's a salad that fits into that category. The combination is unusual and a pleasant surprise.

Peel and dice bananas and combine with diced pineapple. Mix celery, salt, salad dressing, and lemon juice. Fold in fruit, then add drained flaked tuna. Serve on crisp lettuce. Makes 6 to 8 servings.

197. Tuna-stuffed Peppers

4 tablespoons fine dry bread-crumbs
3 tablespoons tarragon vinegar
1 tablespoon capers, drained
¼ teaspoon garlic salt
4 tablespoons mayonnaise
1 tin (7 oz.) tuna, flaked
2 large or 3 medium green peppers
2 tablespoons water
Salad greens

This tuna-filled pepper is seasoned with capers and served with lemon-seasoned mayonnaise.

Combine the breadcrumbs with the vinegar, capers, garlic salt, mayonnaise, and tuna. Cut the green peppers in half, and remove the seeds and veins. Fill the pepper halves with the tuna mixture and arrange them in a casserole or baking dish. Add the 2 tablespoons water to the bottom of the casserole. Bake in a moderate oven (350° F.) for 45–50 minutes, or until the peppers are tender but still hold their shape. Chill until serving time. Serve on a bed of salad greens with lemon mayonnaise. Makes 4 to 6 servings as a salad accompaniment, 2 or 3 as a main course.

LEMON MAYONNAISE: Blend 3 tablespoons lemon juice with ¼ pint mayonnaise.

198. Tuna–Nut Salad

1 package (10 oz.) frozen cut
   green beans
2 cups shredded cabbage
3 tablespoons chopped chives or
   green onions
1 large dill pickle, chopped
2½ oz. chopped walnuts
¼ pint mayonnaise

1 tablespoon light cream
1 teaspoon lemon juice
¼ teaspoon salt
1 small tin (3½ oz.)
   solid pack tuna
2 or 3 hard-boiled eggs, sliced
Lettuce
Minced parsley (optional)

Prepare green beans as directed on package, cooking them until just tender, but still slightly crisp. Drain and chill. Combine the beans with cabbage, chives or onions, dill pickle, and walnuts. Toss. Mix the mayonnaise with cream, lemon juice, and salt. Mix lightly into salad. Drain tuna. Break into large pieces and add to salad with 2 of the sliced eggs. Toss very gently. Arrange in a lettuce-lined bowl or on individual plates. Garnish with hard-boiled egg slices and sprinkle with parsley, if you wish. Makes 6 servings.

199. West Coast Salad

1 large or 2 medium-sized cos
   lettuce
3 shallots, finely minced
1 tin (7 oz.) tuna, flaked
2 hard-boiled eggs, chopped
6 rashers bacon
2 tablespoons vinegar
Pepper

This salad introduces a delicious bacon flavour to a crisp tuna salad.

Wash, dry, and chill lettuce. Tear into pieces in a large bowl. Add shallots, tuna, and eggs. Cook bacon until crisp. Drain and break into bowl, reserving fat. Add vinegar and a few grindings of pepper to bacon fat in same pan. Heat and pour over salad, mixing gently. Taste, and add salt if necessary. Makes 6 servings.

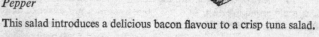

200. Crunchy Tuna Salad

1 tin (7 oz.) tuna, flaked
¼ cup finely chopped onion
3 tablespoons finely chopped
   green pepper
3 tablespoons chopped ripe
   olives
2 tablespoons chopped
   pimiento
½ pint mayonnaise
1 teaspoon garlic vinegar
1 tablespoon light cream
1 tin (3 oz.) crisp Chinese
   noodles
Crisp salad greens for garnish

Chinese noodles are responsible for the crunchiness of this salad. They go in at the last minute so that they will stay crisp. Garnish each serving with two devilled egg halves, if desired.

Combine tuna, onion, green pepper, olives, and pimiento. Blend together the mayonnaise, vinegar, and cream until smooth. Pour over tuna mixture and mix well. Chill. When ready to serve, add crisp noodles and mix lightly. Line a platter or 6 salad plates with salad greens. Spoon on tuna salad. Makes 6 servings.

201. Tuna Appetizer Salad

On individual plates arrange a little curly endive or shredded lettuce. On this put a thick slice of peeled tomato. Top each tomato with half a hard-boiled egg, round side up, and cover all with this tuna mayonnaise: ½ pint mayonnaise combined with ½ cup flaked tuna, and 1 teaspoon lemon juice. Enough for 6 to 8 servings. Garnish each plate with ripe olives if you wish.

Egg, Cheese, Rice, and Pasta Salads

Egg, Cheese, Rice, and Pasta Salads

Egg, cheese, rice, and pasta salads should be given more attention. They make excellent accompaniments to cold cuts and can also be served as main courses at luncheon or supper. When it comes to barbecues, they are also useful as most of them can be prepared well in advance. Many of them actually improve when they are chilled for a while, so that flavours have a chance to blend. They also stand up well if they cannot be served at once.

Most of these salads are hearty. Some can replace an au gratin dish when it is served as an accompaniment to a main course, such as cold meat. I would suggest serving them occasionally in a lettuce-lined casserole instead of a salad bowl.

Feature one of these salads in your next picnic meal. They make a perfect substitute for the usual potato salad. Try them, too, with cold meats in warm-weather meals with hot rolls and butter and a refreshing beverage. Almost any one of the salads in this chapter can be served as the main course at luncheon.

Garnishes are important in this section, for often salads in this group are colourless. A wedge of bright red tomato, strips of pimiento, a sprig of deep green watercress, or a ring of golden pineapple will add a touch of colour as well as a subtle flavour to the following salads.

202. Cheese and Banana Salad

4 large ripe peeled bananas
1 large crisp lettuce
¼ lb. cottage or cream cheese
Salt and paprika to taste
1 heaped teaspoon minced parsley
*   as required*

Remove any threads from bananas. Cut in quarters lengthwise, then across. Line 4 individual plates with crisp lettuce leaves. Divide banana between the plates. Season cheese with salt and paprika. Pipe cheese lightly over the banana in trails. Sprinkle lightly with parsley. Serve with French dressing. Makes 4 servings.

203. Curried Rice Salad

2 cups chilled, boiled rice
1 medium-sized green pepper,
  shredded
2 tablespoons drained pimientos,
  cut in strips
2 tablespoons seedless raisins
2 tablespoons chopped parsley
2 tablespoons chopped spring
  onion
¼ pint olive oil

4 tablespoons wine vinegar
1 tablespoon lemon juice
1 clove garlic, minced or
  mashed
½ tablespoon caster sugar
½–¾ teaspoon curry powder
Salt and pepper to taste
Salad greens
Green pepper rings
Tomato wedges

An ideal accompaniment for barbecued lamb, barbecued or fried chicken, kebabs, or any other grilled meat.

Using two forks, toss together the rice, green pepper, pimientos, raisins, parsley, and onion. Chill thoroughly.
    Combine oil, vinegar, lemon juice, garlic, sugar, curry powder, salt, and pepper. Just before serving, pour over salad and toss thoroughly.
    Arrange salad in a bowl or casserole. Garnish with crisp greens, green pepper rings, and tomato wedges. Makes 4 servings.

204. Double Cheese Salad

1 lb. creamed cottage cheese
3 oz. crumbled Roquefort or
  blue cheese
½ lb. crumbled crisp bacon
2 tablespoons sliced stuffed
  olives
2 tablespoons mayonnaise
Lettuce or curly endive

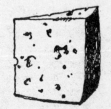

Crumbled, crisp bacon turns cottage cheese and Roquefort, or blue cheese, into a hearty salad with a decisive flavour.

Blend the cottage cheese with the Roquefort or blue cheese, crisp bacon, olives, and mayonnaise. Chill for 1 hour. Serve on crisp lettuce leaves or curly endive. Serves 6.

205. Ham and Cheese Rice Salad

1 package (10 oz.) frozen peas
¾ pint boiling salted water
10 oz. boiled rice
1½ gills mayonnaise
¼ pint chopped dill pickle
1 teaspoon grated onion
Lettuce
1 cup slivered Swiss cheese
1 cup slivered boiled ham
Tomato slices

This salad has some of the heartiness of an oven-baked 'casserole', but you must serve it crisp and cold. It can also stand alone as a main-course luncheon or supper salad.

Add peas to the boiling water. Cover and cook until water boils again. Stir in rice. Cover, remove from heat, and let stand 10 minutes. With a fork, mix in mayonnaise, dill pickle, and grated onion. Chill thoroughly. At serving time, arrange in individual casseroles edged with crisp lettuce, or pile into a lettuce-lined bowl. Top salads with slivers of Swiss cheese and ham. Garnish with tomato slices. Serve with additional mayonnaise. Makes 4 to 6 servings.

206. Year-round Salad

1 medium-sized lettuce
2 peeled bananas
3 hard-boiled eggs
1 tablespoon vinegar
½ teaspoon caster sugar
¾ teaspoon salt
2 tablespoons mayonnaise

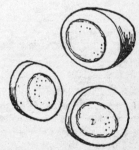

Shred lettuce, slice bananas, and chop eggs coarsely. Toss together with the vinegar, sugar, salt, and mayonnaise. Serve at once. Makes 4 servings.

207. Western Patio Salad

¼ pint vinegar
¼ pint water
1½ oz. caster sugar
1 teaspoon dry mustard
1½ tablespoons flour
¼ teaspoon dry mustard
1½ tablespoons flour

¼ teaspoon each paprika
  and celery salt
¼ teaspoon salt
2 eggs, separated
1 tablespoon butter or margarine
¼ pint single cream
2 cups shell macaroni

Bring vinegar and water to boiling point. Mix the sugar, mustard, flour, paprika, celery salt, salt, and beaten egg yolks together and stir into vinegar and water. Cook until thick. Remove from heat. Add butter. Stir till dissolved. Fold in stiffly beaten egg whites and cream. Cook macaroni as usual in plenty of boiling salted water. Drain, blanch, and mix with hot dressing. Chill salad and serve with a garnish of pimiento or quartered tomatoes. Makes 6 servings.

208. Orange–Macaroni Salad

¼ lb. shell macaroni
Salted water as required
1 knob butter
½ gill mayonnaise
Juice of 1 lemon and orange
2 teaspoons chopped chives
Salt to taste
1 tin (11 oz.) mandarin oranges,
  drained

Place macaroni in a saucepan of boiling salted water to cover. Add butter. Cover and boil for 15–20 minutes until tender, but unbroken. Turn into a colander. Drain and rinse under cold running water. Drain thoroughly. Toss occasionally till cold. Mix the mayonnaise with the lemon and orange juice, chives, and salt to taste. Place macaroni shells and most of the orange sections in a salad bowl. Add dressing. Toss lightly, till blended, with a salad fork and spoon. Garnish with remaining orange sections. Makes 4 servings.

209. Onion and Cheese Salad

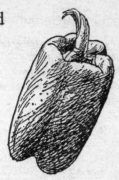

1 large mild onion
¼ lb. Swiss cheese
¼ lb. cooked ham
1 large green pepper
3 tablespoons wine vinegar
4 tablespoons salad oil (part olive
    oil, if desired)
Salt and freshly ground
    pepper to taste
Crisp lettuce

Slice onion very thinly, cut slices in half, separate rings, and cover with
ice water. Chill for about 2 hours. Cut into match-like pieces Swiss
cheese, ham, and green pepper. Combine with drained onion. Stir in
vinegar, salad oil, salt, and pepper. Chill. Serve on lettuce. Makes 6
servings.

210. Stuffed Pimiento Salad

2 cups boiled macaroni
¼ cup crushed pineapple,
    drained
1 medium-sized tomato, diced
½ teaspoon salt
Dash of pepper
2 teaspoons prepared mustard
3 tablespoons soured cream
4 teaspoons wine vinegar
1 teaspoon scraped onion
8 oz. whole pimientos
Crisp lettuce

Bright red pimientos are used as containers for a fruit-flavoured macaroni salad. This salad is good with cold slices of turkey or fried chicken.
Combine the cooked macaroni with the drained pineapple, tomato,
salt, and pepper. Mix together the mustard, soured cream, wine vinegar,
and onion. Toss this dressing with the macaroni mixture. Drain the
whole pimientos and stuff each with the macaroni salad. Serve on a bed
of lettuce. Surround with spring onions if you wish. Makes 4 to 6 servings.

211. Barbecue Salad Bowl

1 jar (2 oz.) stuffed green olives
½ pint mayonnaise
3 tablespoons wine vinegar
2 teaspoons caster sugar
1 teaspoon chilli powder
Pinch of cayenne
½ teaspoon salt
¼ teaspoon pepper
14 oz. shell macaroni, boiled
    and drained

1 tin (1 lb.) garbanzos,
    if available
1 tin (7 oz.) tuna, flaked
3 oz. seedless raisins (optional)
1 dill pickle, chopped
1 spring onion, sliced
2 tablespoons chopped parsley
1 clove garlic, minced or mashed
Crisp salad greens
1½ tablespoons capers

Pasta salads take many forms, but I think this is a most unusual one. The raisins add sweetness to the rather tart salad combination.

Drain liquid from olives (retain olives for use later), and combine with mayonnaise, vinegar, sugar, chilli powder, cayenne, salt, and pepper. Toss dressing with macaroni, garbanzos, tuna, raisins, pickle, onions, parsley, and garlic. Heap into a salad bowl lined with crisp greens; garnish with halved stuffed olives and capers. Makes 8 servings.

NOTE: If garbanzos are not available, substitute boiled green peas.

Moulded and Frozen Salads

Moulded and Frozen Salads

Moulded and frozen salads are, for the most part, quite simple to make yet, with a little trouble, they can present a very festive picture. Setting salad ingredients in a shimmering sparkling jelly, or in a creamy smooth base, seems to give them a new personality. Even the simple moulded or frozen salad takes on a special party air. Another point in their favour is that they can be prepared well ahead.

In deciding which moulded or frozen salad is to be included in a meal, consider the other courses. The rich, mousse-type of salad is hearty fare and so should be served with simple dishes. Many salads in this chapter are suitable for dessert salads. Spicy salads, in convivial moods, make good accompaniments to cold meat.

Salad moulds are obtainable in various shapes and sizes, but many other containers, such as freezer cartons or loaf or muffin tins, make satisfactory moulds. To measure the capacity of a container, simply measure the amount of water required to fill it.

When salad is ready to mould, dip mould in cold water, or brush lightly with cooking oil, then add.

To unmould a salad, first loosen the mould by running the tip of a flexible knife around the edge of the salad, then dip the mould quickly in warm water. Place a serving dish on top and invert quickly. Remove the mould, and then garnish the salad to taste.

212. Frozen Avocado Moulds

½ pint sieved avocado pulp
3 tablespoons lime juice
3 tablespoons salad oil
½ teaspoon salt
2 tablespoons finely grated
    Cheddar cheese
1 tin (9 oz.) sliced pineapple
Lettuce

Mix thoroughly avocado pulp, lime juice, oil, salt, and cheese. Spoon into 4 moulds and pat down with back of spoon. Freeze until firm. Arrange pineapple slices on lettuce. Dip moulds in lukewarm water and turn out a frozen mould on to each slice of pineapple. Makes 4 servings.

213. Washington Apple Salad

1 tablespoon cinnamon-flavoured
   candies
¼ pint plus 2 tablespoons water
3 oz. packaged lemon jelly
½ pint apple purée
8 oz. small curd cottage cheese,
   forced through a fine wire
   strainer

1 cup diced unpeeled red apples
¾ cup finely chopped celery
1½ oz. chopped walnuts
2 tablespoons mayonnaise
¼ pint ice cold evaporated milk
2 teaspoons lemon juice
Salad greens

To cut back on calories, cottage cheese and evaporated milk are used instead of the more typical cream cheese and whipping cream.

Boil together candies and water, stirring until candies are dissolved. Remove from heat. Add jelly and stir until dissolved. Blend in apple purée and cottage cheese. Chill until syrupy. Stir in apples, celery, walnuts, and mayonnaise. Combine evaporated milk and lemon juice and whip until stiff. Fold into jelly mixture. Pour into a 2-quart mould and chill until set. Turn out on to a platter lined with salad greens, and serve. Makes 6 servings.

214. Avocado Cheese Aspic

3 oz. packaged lime jelly
¾ pint hot water
6 oz. cream cheese
2 tablespoons light cream or milk
1 tablespoon lemon juice
1 teaspoon onion juice
Few drops of Worcester sauce
   and Tabasco

1 teaspoon salt
1 cup finely diced avocado
1 cup finely sliced celery
2 tablespoons finely chopped
   pimiento
Crisp lettuce
3 or 4 hard-boiled eggs, cut
   in quarters lengthwise

This pale green moulded salad, flecked with bits of pimiento, is an attractive addition to a party buffet or luncheon. The base is a rather sweet blend of cream cheese and lime jelly.

Dissolve jelly in hot water and chill until syrupy. Blend together cream cheese, cream or milk, lemon juice, onion juice, salt, Worcester sauce, and Tabasco. Add to dissolved jelly and mix well. Fold in avocado, celery, and pimiento. Pour into a 1½-quart mould and chill until firm. Unmould on to a bed of lettuce. Border with egg quarters. Makes 10 servings.

215. Moulded Guacamole Ring

2 envelopes (2 tablespoons)
unflavoured gelatine
¼ pint cold water
Boiling water as required
6 tablespoons lemon or lime juice
1½ teaspoons grated onion
2¼ teaspoons salt
Dash of Tabasco
1½ pints mashed avocados,
(approximately 3 large avocados)
1¼ gills mayonnaise

This salad, held together lightly by jelly, tastes like a very good guacamole. Fill the ring with shrimp, crab, or chicken salad. To be at its best, it should be eaten the day it is made, for when it stands any longer, it turns brown around the edges.

Soften gelatine in cold water and dissolve in enough boiling water to make 1 pint. Add lemon or lime juice, onion, and seasonings. Peel and mash avocados. While gelatine mixture is still liquid, stir in avocado pulp. Fold in mayonnaise. Pour into 10-inch ring mould and chill until firm. Unmould and fill centre with chilled seafood or chicken salad. Makes 8 servings.

216. Gingered Grape and Pear Mould

¼ pint hot water
3 oz. packaged lemon jelly
½ pint ginger ale
1 cup diced fresh pears
1 oz. chopped pecans (toasted, if desired)

3 oz. halved seeded grapes
2 teaspoons finely chopped crystallized ginger
Salad greens
Mayonnaise or other salad dressing

Ginger ale and crystallized ginger add a special spiciness to this amber-coloured jellied fruit salad.

Pour hot water over jelly in a bowl, and stir until dissolved. Cool. Stir in ginger ale and chill until syrupy. Mix together the pears, grapes, nuts, and ginger, and stir into the jelly mixture. Turn into a 1-quart ring mould or 6 individual moulds. Chill until firm. Unmould on salad greens. Serve with a bowl of mayonnaise in the centre of the ring. Makes 6 servings.

217. Avocado and Tomato Salad Mould

You mould an avocado-sour cream aspic on top of a tomato aspic for this light green and red salad.

AVOCADO ASPIC:
1 envelope (1 tablespoon)
    unflavoured gelatine
¼ gill cold water
½ pint boiling water
1 teaspoon caster sugar
2 tablespoons lemon juice
½ pint mashed avocado (1 large)
¼ pint each soured cream and
    mayonnaise
1 teaspoon salt
Pepper and dash of cayenne

Soften gelatine in cold water, pour in boiling water, and stir until dissolved. Add sugar and 1 tablespoon of the lemon juice. Chill until slightly thickened. Immediately after mashing avocado, add the other tablespoon lemon juice, soured cream, mayonnaise, salt, pepper, and cayenne. Mix thoroughly with chilled jelly. Pour into 2-quart mould. Chill until set.

TOMATO ASPIC:
1 envelope (1 tablespoon)
    unflavoured gelatine
¼ gill cold water
½ pint boiling water less
    2 tablespoons
1 tablespoon caster sugar
1 tin (10 oz.) tomato soup
1 tablespoon lemon juice
¼ teaspoon salt
Salad greens

Soften gelatine in cold water. Dissolve in boiling water. Add sugar, soup, lemon juice, and salt. Pour over firm avocado aspic. Chill until set. Unmould on to a platter lined with salad greens. Makes 8 to 10 servings.

218. Cherry Salad

1 tin (1 lb. 13 oz.) sweet dark
  cherries (stoned if available)
4 tablespoons lemon juice
Water
3 oz. packaged orange jelly
3 oz. coarsely chopped pecans
3 oz. pimiento-stuffed green olives
Crisp lettuce
Mayonnaise or sour-cream dressing

Drain the syrup from the cherries into a pint measuring cup. Add the lemon juice and enough water to give you 3½ gills of liquid. Turn into a saucepan, heat, pour over jelly, and stir until the jelly is completely dissolved. Let chill until syrupy.

While mixture is chilling, stone cherries (if necessary). If you prefer very crisp nuts, toast the pecans in a moderate oven for a few minutes. Drain the olives and cut in slices. When jelly is ready, add the cherries, pecans, and olives. Turn into a 1½-quart mould or individual moulds. Chill until firm. Unmould and garnish with lettuce. Serve with mayonnaise or a sour cream dressing. Makes 8 servings.

219. Melon Mould with Cherries

1 tin (1 lb. 13 oz.) cherries
1 tin (1 lb. 4 oz.) pineapple titbits
Water
3 oz. packaged lemon jelly
1 medium-sized cantaloup
Fresh mint
Melon balls for garnish

Melon cubes go into the jellied base of this moulded salad, and melon balls garnish the salad after it is turned out of the mould.

Drain juice from cherries and pineapple titbits. Measure, and add enough water to make 1 cup of each. Dissolve jelly in the pineapple juice. Stir in cherry juice. Chill until syrupy. Halve, seed, and peel cantaloup, and cut into small cubes. Place melon cubes in bottom of a 1½-quart ring mould. Add pineapple and cherries to chilled jelly. Pour over melon cubes. Chill until firm. Unmould on to a bed of fresh mint and garnish with melon balls. Makes 8 servings.

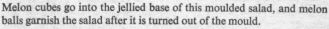

220. Cranberry and Orange Relish Salad

1½ lb. raw cranberries
8–12 oz. caster sugar
4 envelopes (4 tablespoons)
 unflavoured gelatine
½ pint orange juice
2 cups chopped celery
3 oz. chopped walnuts
Curly endive
Mayonnaise (optional)

This tart, crisp, moulded salad can replace the usual cranberry relish as an accompaniment to roast turkey at Christmas time.

Mince cranberries, using a fine blade. Mix in sugar and let stand about 15 minutes, stirring occasionally. Meanwhile, soften gelatine in orange juice. Stir over hot water until dissolved. Combine cranberry and orange mixtures. Add celery and walnuts. Pour into 12 individual moulds (8 oz. size). Chill until set, preferably overnight. Unmould salads on to individual salad plates lined with curly endive. Serve with mayonnaise if desired. Makes 12 servings.

221. Moulded Grape Salad

1 lb. grapes
1½ gills French dressing
1 pint hot water less 2 tablespoons
3 oz. packaged lemon jelly
5 tablespoons orange juice
3 tablespoons lemon juice
½ teaspoon finely chopped onion
¼ teaspoon salt
3 oz. cream cheese
Crisp lettuce

Wash, slit, and seed grapes. (Reserve 12 grape halves.) Marinate remainder in French dressing 30 minutes. Drain. (Save dressing for later use.) Pour hot water over jelly and stir until dissolved. Stir in orange juice, lemon juice, onion, and salt. Chill until jelly mixture mounds slightly when dropped from a spoon. Stir in marinated grapes. Spoon into 6 individual moulds or a 1 quart mould. Chill until set. Soften cheese and form into 6 balls. Place each ball between 2 of the remaining grape halves. Unmould salad on to a bed of lettuce, and garnish with cheese balls. A mixture of half mayonnaise and half whipped cream may be served as a dressing. Makes 6 servings.

222. Jellied Melon Salad

1 tablespoon (1 envelope)
   unflavoured gelatine
¼ gill cold water
2 tablespoons lemon juice
¼ pint ginger ale
4 cups small cantaloup
   balls or cubes
2 cups small water-melon
   balls or cubes
6 or 8 rings (about 1 inch thick)
   honeydew melon

FRUIT–CHEESE DRESSING:
6 oz. creamed cottage cheese
1½ tablespoons lemon juice
3 tablespoons orange juice
1 teaspoon each lemon peel and
   orange peel
1½ tablespoons honey

This tangy, colourful melon salad has a low-calorie dressing.

Soften the gelatine in cold water. Stir over hot water until thoroughly dissolved. Add the lemon juice and ginger ale and stir until well blended. Combine the cantaloup and water-melon and arrange in the bottom of 6 or 8 individual salad moulds or a 2-quart salad mould or square baking tin. Pour the gelatine mixture over melon balls. Chill until firm. Unmould or cut in squares. Arrange each serving on a melon ring. To make the dressing, combine all ingredients and whirl smooth in electric blender, or press cottage cheese through strainer and whip with remaining ingredients. Makes 6 to 8 servings.

223. Orange–Sour Cream Mould

3 oz. packaged lemon jelly
¼ pint orange juice
1 tin (11 oz.) mandarin orange
   sections

2 tablespoons lemon juice
1 lb. seedless grapes
¼ pint soured cream

This moulded salad includes juicy mandarin orange segments and seedless grapes.

Dissolve jelly in heated orange juice. Stir in lemon juice. Chill until syrupy. Drain liquid from the mandarin orange sections. (Save the liquid for punch or other moulded salads.) Fold the soured cream and the drained fruits into the jelly, turn into 6 moulds, and chill until firm. Makes 6 servings.

NOTE: Freshly extracted peach juice or tinned papaya juice may be used in place of orange juice.

224. Mandarin Orange Salad Mould with Fruited Cream

3 oz. packaged lemon jelly
¼ pint hot water less 2 tablespoons
¼ pint cold water less 2 tablespoons
2 tablespoons lemon juice
¼ pint orange juice concentrate
2 tins (11 oz. each) mandarin
  oranges, drained

DRESSING:
1 peeled banana
1 tin (9 oz.) crushed pineapple,
  well drained
¼ pint mayonnaise
¼ pint whipping cream
Curly endive

The dressing of puréed banana, crushed pineapple, and whipped cream doubles the fruit flavour of the delicious fruit jelly.

Dissolve jelly in the hot water. Stir in cold water, lemon juice, orange juice, and the mandarin oranges. When about to set, stir and turn into a 1½-quart salad mould and let chill until firm. For the dressing mash the banana and mix with the crushed pineapple and mayonnaise. Whip cream until stiff, and fold in. Turn into a sauce boat. Unmould salad on to a bed of crisp endive or other greens, and pass the dressing separately. Makes about 8 servings.

225. Moulded Peach Salad

3 oz. packaged lemon jelly
2½ gills hot water
3 medium-sized ripe
  peaches
Watercress or crisp salad
  greens
Soured cream or mayonnaise
Slivered almonds, if desired

Dissolve jelly in hot water. Chill until syrupy. Peel peaches and force pulp through a sieve. Blend pulp with jelly mixture and pour into 5 or 6 individual moulds or a 1½-pint mould. Chill until firm. Dip moulds quickly in warm water and unmould on watercress. Serve with soured cream or mayonnaise, topped with almonds, if desired. Makes 5 or 6 servings.

PINEAPPLE VARIATION:

Drain and save syrup from 1 tin (8 oz.) crushed pineapple. Add enough water to make 2½ gills. Bring to the boil. Proceed as directed above, adding crushed pineapple along with peach pulp to jelly mixture.

226. Lime–Lemon–Orange Layered Salad

This unusual combination of fruits and vegetables has a sour cream layer in the centre.

FIRST LAYER:
3 oz. packaged lime jelly
1 pint hot water less 2 tablespoons
2 coarsely grated carrots
3 stalks celery, finely sliced
1 medium-sized avocado, cubed

Dissolve jelly in the water. Chill until it is syrupy, then fold in carrots, celery, and avocado. Turn into two 4 by 12-inch loaf tins or one 9 by 14-inch baking dish. Chill until firm.

SECOND LAYER:
3 oz. packaged lemon jelly
Hot water as required
½ pint soured cream
2 peeled bananas

Prepare lemon jelly, using ½ pint hot water (less 2 tablespoons). Cool. Stir in soured cream, blending well. Slice bananas and fold in. Turn out over the firm lime jelly layer, and chill until firm.

THIRD LAYER:
1 tin (1 lb. 13 oz.) apricot halves
Water
6 oz. packaged orange jelly
1 pint cold water less 4 tablespoons
¾ lb. seedless grapes
Salad greens

Drain juice from apricots and measure juice. Add enough water to make ¾ pint liquid. Heat to boiling point. Add jelly, and stir until dissolved. Stir in cold water. Chill until syrupy. Stir in washed grapes and the apricot halves. Turn out over the sour-cream layer, and chill overnight.

Turn out on a platter lined with crisp salad greens. Makes 16 servings.

227. Orange–Pineapple–Apricot Salad Ring

This tart, fruit-filled salad is especially eye-catching.

FIRST LAYER:
1 package orange jelly
Hot water as required

Dissolve jelly in enough hot water to make 1 pint. Pour into a 3 quart ring mould, and chill until firm.

SECOND LAYER:
2 envelopes (2 tablespoons)
  unflavoured gelatine
6 tablespoons lemon juice
1 tin (1 lb. 4 oz.) crushed
  pineapple
¼ teaspoon salt
1½ large packages cream
  cheese
½ pint mayonnaise
2 teaspoons grated horse-
  radish
1 cup finely sliced celery
½ pint whipping cream

Soften gelatine in lemon juice. Drain juice from the pineapple, and add enough water to make 2½ gills; heat to boiling, and add softened gelatine. Stir until dissolved. Stir in salt. Chill until syrupy. Cream the cream cheese until light, and beat in the mayonnaise and horseradish. Blend into the chilled jelly. Fold in crushed pineapple and celery. Whip cream until stiff, and fold in. Spread over orange layer and chill until firm.

THIRD LAYER:
2 envelopes (2 tablespoons)
  unflavoured gelatine
1 can (1 lb. 13 oz.) apricot
  halves
Juice of 1 lemon
  (3 tablespoons juice)
3 tablespoons cold water
Juice of 2 oranges (barely
  1¼ gills juice)
4 oz. blanched almonds,
  finely chopped
Salad greens (optional)

Soften gelatine in cold water. Drain juice from apricots, and add enough water to make ½ pint. Heat to boiling, add softened gelatine, and stir until dissolved. Stir in lemon juice and orange juice. Chill until syrupy. Chop apricots and stir in. Add chopped almonds. Carefully spoon over the firm pineapple layer. Let chill overnight. Turn out on a platter, lined with greens if liked. Makes 16 servings.

228. Double-decker Pineapple–Cherry Salad

Sandwiched between this double-decker fruit mould is a thin layer of cream cheese. Olives contrast pleasingly with the juicy sweet cherries and bits of pineapple.

FIRST LAYER:
1 tin (1 lb. 4 oz.) sliced
  pineapple
Water
3 oz. packaged cherry jelly

Drain pineapple. Add enough water to the syrup to make a good ¾ pint liquid. Heat liquid to boiling point. Dissolve jelly in the hot liquid. Chill until syrupy. Cut pineapple slices into ¼-inch pieces and stir into the jelly mixture. Turn into an 8-inch square tin. Let chill until firm.

SECOND LAYER:
3 oz. cream cheese
2 tablespoons light cream

Let cream cheese warm to room temperature. Mix it with the light cream until light and fluffy. Spread over the jelly and chill until firm.

THIRD LAYER:
1 tin (1 lb.) stoned cherries
4 tablespoons lemon juice
1 tablespoon orange juice
Water
3 oz. packaged orange jelly
¼ pint sliced stuffed olives
Salad greens

Drain cherries. Add lemon and orange juice to cherry syrup and then enough water to make ¾ pint liquid. Heat to boiling point. Add jelly, and stir until dissolved. Chill until syrupy. Add cherries and sliced olives, and pour over the cream cheese mixture. Chill overnight. Unmould on a bed of crisp greens. Serves 8 to 10.

229. Pineapple, Kumquat, and Pomegranate Salad

3 tablespoons sherry or port wine
2 cups diced fresh pineapple
1 cup pomegranate seeds
¼ cup seeded and thinly sliced
   preserved kumquats
3 oz. cream cheese
2 tablespoons each kumquat
   and lemon juice
¼ teaspoon seasoned salt
¾ teaspoon dry mustard
1¼ tablespoons caster sugar
¾ pint whipping cream
Salad greens

Pour sherry or port over pineapple, pomegranate seeds, and kumquats. Meanwhile, blend cream cheese with kumquat syrup, lemon juice, seasoned salt, dry mustard, and sugar. Add cream and whip until stiff. Fold in fruit and wine. Turn into two 1-quart refrigerator trays and freeze until firm. Cut and serve on bed of greens or from a chilled pineapple shell. Makes 8 to 10 servings.

230. Blueberry Salad Mould

1¼ cups fresh, tinned, or
   frozen blueberries
¼ pint water or blueberry
   juice less 2 tablespoons
2 tablespoons cornflour

Pinch of salt
1 saltspoon grated nutmeg
¼ teaspoon cinnamon
2 oz. caster sugar
3 oz. packaged lemon jelly

Combine blueberries with liquid and bring to the boil. Mix together cornflour, salt, spices, and sugar. Add to blueberries gradually and cook until thick, stirring constantly. Prepare lemon jelly as directed on package. Pour half of the jelly into a mould and let it get firm. Mix the remaining jelly into the blueberry mixture and pour on the top of the firm jelly. Chill until set. Makes 6 to 8 servings.

231. Moulded Strawberry Ring

3 oz. packaged strawberry jelly
Hot water as required
6 oz. cream cheese
4 tablespoons light cream
½ teaspoon salt
2 oz. finely chopped nuts
1 lb. strawberries

A festive dinner salad: whole fresh strawberries and nut-filled cream cheese balls in a shimmering strawberry jelly mould. For an extra garnish, fill the centre of the ring mould with banana fool.

Dissolve jelly in enough hot water to make ¾ pint. Pour a thin layer of the jelly into the bottom of a 1½-quart ring mould. Chill until set. Chill remaining jelly until syrupy. Meanwhile, blend cheese, cream, salt, and nuts. Form into 12 balls. Wash and hull berries, and select the largest to place inside ring mould. Alternate berries and cheese balls in mould. Carefully pour remaining jelly over berries and cheese, and chill till set. Turn out on to a platter and garnish with remaining berries. Makes 8 servings.

232. Strawberry–Blueberry Mould

1½ pints water
6 oz. packaged cherry jelly
2 punnets strawberries
(approximately 1 lb.)

3 tablespoons pale dry sherry
1 package frozen blueberries,
practically thawed
1½–2 lb. seeded grapes

Heat 1 pint of the water. Add jelly and stir until dissolved. Stir in the remaining water and the wine. Chill until syrupy. Wash and halve strawberries, and arrange in the bottom of a 3-quart ring mould, or use individual moulds. Pour in enough of the chilled jelly to cover berries. Chill. Mix the remaining jelly with blueberries and grapes, and pour into mould. Chill until firm. When ready to serve, unmould on to a platter. If liked, fringe base with blackcurrant, raspberry, or strawberry leaves. Makes 10 to 12 servings.

233. Artichoke Ring

6–8 boiled globe artichokes
1 envelope (1 tablespoon)
   unflavoured gelatine
3 tablespoons cold water
¼ pint boiling water
3 tablespoons lemon juice

Garlic to taste
¼ teaspoon salt
¼ teaspoon paprika
¼ pint whipping cream
½ pint mayonnaise

For more flavour, add a clove of garlic to the water in which you cook the artichokes for this moulded salad. Strips of pimiento crisscrossed over the artichoke ring make it even more attractive.

Scrape all the tender meat from the artichoke leaves and cut the hearts into quarters. Soften gelatine in cold water and then dissolve in boiling water. Add lemon juice and seasonings. Cool until slightly thickened. Whip cream and fold into mixture along with mayonnaise and artichoke pulp and hearts. Pour into an 8-inch ring mould and chill until firm. Unmould and fill the centre with chilled, cooked vegetables, tomato quarters, or avocado and shrimp marinated in French dressing. Makes 8 to 10 servings.

234. Beetroot and Olive Salad

6 oz. packaged lemon jelly
½ pint hot water
½ pint cold water
1 tin (1 lb.) shredded beetroot
12 pimiento-stuffed green olives
   chopped

½ cup chopped sweet pickles
1 tablespoon each onion salt
   and garlic salt
Crisp lettuce
French dressing as required

This is spicy, with chopped sweet pickles and pimiento-stuffed green olives.

Dissolve jelly in hot water. Stir in cold water. Drain beetroot. Add beetroot liquid to dissolved jelly. Chill until syrupy. Blend in beetroot, olives, and pickles. Season with onion and garlic salt. Pour into an 8-inch square tin or individual moulds. Chill until firm. Unmould salad on to a dish lined with lettuce. Serve with French dressing. Makes 8 to 10 servings.

235. Borsch Jellied Salad

1 tin (10¼ oz.) consommé
Water
3 oz. packaged lemon jelly
1½ tablespoons vinegar
¼ pint shredded tinned beetroot
1 cup finely shredded cabbage
1 tablespoon grated onion
1 teaspoon salt
Dash of pepper
Shredded lettuce
Sour cream dressing

Crisp cabbage and firm beetroot give an interesting texture to this consommé-flavoured jellied salad.

Heat consommé and enough water to make 3½ gills liquid. Pour over jelly and stir until dissolved. Add vinegar. Chill until syrupy. Stir in beetroot, cabbage, onion, salt, and pepper. Turn mixture into an 8-inch square tin. Chill until firm. Unmould salad on to shredded lettuce. Top with dressing. Makes 6 to 8 servings.

236. Tomato Fruit Jelly

¾ pint tomato juice
3 oz. packaged raspberry jelly
1 tablespoon cold water
¼ tablespoon caster sugar
¼ teaspoon salt
2 tablespoons cider vinegar
* or lemon juice*

½ cup chopped cucumber
½ cup chopped celery
3 tablespoons minced spring
* onion*
Mayonnaise or sour-cream
* dressing*
Salad greens

Bring ½ pint of the tomato juice to the boil. Add the jelly, and stir until thoroughly dissolved. Add the remaining tomato juice, water, sugar, salt, and vinegar or lemon juice. Chill until the mixture begins to thicken. Stir in the cucumber, celery, and spring onion. Turn into a 1-quart mould or into 4 or 5 individual moulds. Chill until firm. Unmould and serve with mayonnaise or sour cream dressing. Garnish the salad plates with crisp greens. Makes 4 or 5 servings.

237. Moulded Gazpacho Salad

1 envelope (1 tablespoon)
  unflavoured gelatine
About 2½ gills tomato juice
1 large ripe tomato
2 tablespoons vinegar or pickle
  juice
1 medium-sized cucumber,
  chopped

1 saltspoon crushed garlic
1 peeled and seeded green pepper,
  chopped
3 tablespoons chopped onion
About ½ teaspoon salt
1 saltspoon freshly ground pepper
Crisp salad greens

The ingredients usually used in the Spanish cold soup, *gazpacho*, are used here in the moulded salad. It makes a very nice summer meal followed by cold cuts and hot rolls.

Soften the gelatine in ½ gill of the tomato juice for about 5 minutes. Meanwhile heat ¼ pint of the tomato juice. Add the gelatine and stir until thoroughly dissolved. Chop the fresh tomato, saving the juice. Add vinegar and remaining tomato juice to make ¼ pint liquid. Add to the hot mixture with the garlic, cucumber, green pepper, onion, salt and pepper. Pour into a 1-quart mould. Chill until firm. Unmould on a bed of crisp greens. Makes 4 to 6 servings.

238. Moulded Baked Bean Salad

3 oz. packaged lemon jelly
½ pint boiling water
3 tablespoons tomato ketchup
3 tablespoons tarragon vinegar
2 teaspoons horseradish
¼ teaspoon Tabasco

2 cups tinned baked beans
2 tablespoons each chopped
  green onion and dill pickle
¼ cup sliced celery
Crisp lettuce
French dressing as required

A jellied baked bean salad rates as a novelty in the category of moulded salads. In this one, crisp onion, pickle, and celery provide a contrast to the soft beans.

Dissolve the jelly in boiling water. Add ketchup, vinegar, horseradish, and Tabasco. Chill until syrupy. Mix in beans, onion, pickle, and celery, and pour into loaf tin, 1 quart ring mould, or 8 individual moulds. Chill until set. Turn out of mould on to a plate lined with lettuce leaves, and serve with a sharp French dressing to which a few capers may be added. Makes 8 servings.

239. Ham and Tongue Aspic

ASPIC:
3 tins (10¼ oz. each) consommé
¼ pint water
1 medium-sized onion, sliced
2 stalks celery, sliced
2 envelopes (2 tablespoons)
  unflavoured gelatine

Bring to the boil the consommé and 1¼ gills water. Add onion and celery. Cover and simmer 15 minutes. Strain and save liquid. To hot consommé add gelatine softened in ¼ pint water. Stir until dissolved. Pour into a 1½-or 2-quart mould, and set mould in ice water that is just a little deeper than the top level of mixture. Let stand until a layer of aspic about ¼ inch thick has coated sides of mould. Pour out liquid centre and save

FILLING:
Hard-boiled egg slices
Cooked ox tongue slices
¾ lb. diced cooked ham
2 hard-boiled eggs, diced
⅔ cup chopped celery
1 spring onion, minced
2 tablespoons finely chopped
  pimiento
Crisp lettuce
Mayonnaise
Prepared mustard

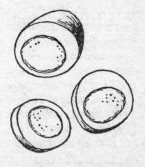

Decorate aspic shell with slices of egg, dipped first in aspic, then attached to sides and bottom. Let chill until eggs hold securely. Pour a little of the aspic (if it gets thick, set in hot water and stir) into mould, and line with slices of cooked ox tongue. Let chill while you combine with remaining aspic the ham, eggs, celery, onion, and pimiento. Fill mould and chill at least 4 hours or overnight. Unmould on lettuce. Cut and serve with a dressing of mayonnaise flavoured to taste with prepared mustard. Makes 8 to 10 servings.

240. Potato Salad Roll

4 cups cubed boiled potatoes
½ cup finely sliced celery
2–3 tablespoons finely chopped
  sweet pickle
2 tablespoons finely chopped parsley
2 tablespoons finely chopped
  pimiento

4 hard-boiled eggs, chopped
1 tablespoon grated onion
¾ teaspoon salt
1 tablespoon lemon juice
1½ gills mayonnaise or salad
  dressing
Relishes for garnish (optional)

When well chilled, this salad roll slices neatly. Frost the top with mayonnaise, and garnish with pimiento and parsley, if you wish to dress it up a little.

Toss together the potatoes, celery, sweet pickle, parsley, pimiento, and egg. Add the onion, salt, lemon juice, and mayonnaise. Mix thoroughly. Turn salad out on to a large piece of aluminium foil and shape into a roll, approximately 8 by 4 by 2½ inches. Roll up in foil. Chill 24 hours. Turn out on a platter and garnish with radish roses, stoned ripe olives, and tomato wedges, if desired. Cut in slices to serve. Makes 8 servings.

241. Turkey Mousse

1 envelope (1 tablespoon)
  unflavoured gelatine
4 tablespoons cold water
2½ gills well-seasoned turkey or
  chicken stock or 2 chicken
  bouillon cubes dissolved in 2½
  gills hot water
1 lb. diced, cooked turkey

½ cup sliced celery
½ cup cooked peas
½ cup mayonnaise
3 tablespoons each chopped
  pimiento, pickle relish, and
  slivered blanched almonds
Crisp salad greens

This moulded salad is almost a complete meal because it contains a large amount of turkey, celery, and peas. It is a colourful salad to feature at a buffet supper, or, if you wish to have it as the main course for Sunday supper, serve it with hot tomato soup and plenty of hot rolls.

Soften gelatine in cold water. Heat turkey stock. Add gelatine, and stir until it dissolves. Chill until syrupy, then fold in the turkey meat, celery, peas, mayonnaise, pimiento, pickle relish, and almonds. Turn into a 2-quart mould. Chill until firm, at least 3 to 4 hours. Unmould on a platter and garnish with crisp greens before serving. Makes 8 servings.

242. Cream of Chicken Mousse

1 tin (10½ oz.) cream of chicken
soup
1 tin of water
2 envelopes (2 tablespoons)
unflavoured gelatine
1½ gills cold water
4 tablespoons mayonnaise
1 tin (6 oz.) minced chicken or
turkey or ¾ cup leftover fowl

¼ pint, double cream, whipped
2 oz. sliced, stuffed olives
1 large stalk celery, thinly sliced
1 tablespoon lemon juice
¼ teaspoon salt
Paprika to taste
Crisp lettuce
Parsley

Pour soup into pan, fill tin with water, and blend into soup until smooth.
Heat to boiling point. Soften gelatine in cold water and stir into soup.
Cool until it begins to thicken. Mix in mayonnaise and blend thoroughly.
Fold in whipped cream. Add remaining ingredients. Chill in 8 individual
moulds. When set, unmould on lettuce and garnish with parsley. If
dressing is desired, thin mayonnaise with tarragon vinegar, or use a tart
French dressing. Makes 8 servings.

243. Moulded Prawn Salad

1 tablespoon (1 envelope)
unflavoured gelatine
1½ gills water
¾ pint yogurt
¼ pint tomato ketchup
½ teaspoon salt
¼ teaspoon dill seed
1 pint diced boiled prawns
Cucumber slices

Yogurt is the creamy base of this rich, tasty prawn salad.

Soften gelatine in ½ gill of the water. Add remaining water, heated to
boiling point, and stir till dissolved. Blend in yogurt, ketchup, salt, and
dill seed. Chill until syrupy. Stir in prawns and pour mixture into a 2-
quart mould. Chill until set, in about 3 hours. Unmould on to serving
dish and garnish with cucumber slices. Makes 6 to 8 servings.

244. Curry Ring with Chicken Salad

This luncheon salad can be prepared a day in advance for an easy buffet meal to serve to a large group. You fill the centre of the ring mould with a festive salad of chicken, celery, fresh pineapple, and salted almonds.

1½ envelopes (1½ tablespoons)
   unflavoured gelatine
¼ pint dry white table wine
1 pint chicken stock
2 teaspoons curry powder
½ pint mayonnaise
1 tablespoon finely chopped
   spring onion
1 cup finely sliced celery
1 finely chopped pimiento
1 teaspoon salt
3 hard-boiled eggs, chopped
3 tablespoons each sliced ripe
   olives and stuffed green olives
Crisp salad greens

Soften gelatine in cold wine. Heat ½ pint of the chicken stock with the curry powder to boiling point. Add gelatine and stir until dissolved. Stir in ½ pint cold stock and chill until syrupy. Fold in mayonnaise, then mix in spring onion, celery, pimiento, salt, eggs, and olives. Turn into an oiled 1½-quart ring mould or 8 individual ring moulds. Chill until firm.

    Unmould ring mould on a bed of greens and fill the centre of the ring with the chicken salad. Makes 8 generous servings.

CHICKEN SALAD :

3 cups diced, boiled chicken
1 cup finely sliced celery
1 tablespoon grated onion
1 tablespoon lemon juice
¼ teaspoon salt

Dash of cayenne
¼ pint mayonnaise
½ cup slivered salted almonds
1 cup fresh pineapple pieces
   (optional)

    Toss together the diced chicken, celery, onion, lemon juice, salt, and cayenne. Chill several hours. When ready to serve, blend in mayonnaise, almonds, and pineapple.

245. Frosted Salmon Mousse

1 tin (1 lb.) flaked red salmon
1 envelope (1 tablespoon)
  unflavoured gelatine
¼ gill cold water
¼ gill boiling water
2 tablespoons each lemon juice
  and vinegar

½ teaspoon salt
½ tablespoon caster sugar
2 teaspoons grated onion
1 teaspoon horseradish
3 tablespoons sliced ripe olives
¼ cup finely sliced celery
¾ pint mayonnaise

Remove skin and bones from salmon. In a medium-sized bowl, soften gelatine in cold water. Add boiling water and stir until dissolved. Mix in salt, lemon juice, vinegar, sugar, grated onion, and horseradish. Cool until slightly thickened. Stir in salmon, olives, celery, and mayonnaise. Turn into a 5- by 9-inch oiled loaf tin and chill until firm. Turn out on to a platter and frost with avocado spread.

AVOCADO SPREAD:
Combine ¼ pint sieved avocado, about ½ gill soured cream, ⅔ teaspoon salt, and a dash of cayenne. Frost top of salmon loaf with mixture. Hand remainder of avocado spread separately.

246. Moulded Sardine Ring

1 envelope (1 tablespoon)
  unflavoured gelatine
¾ pint water
2 bouillon cubes
2 teaspoons lemon juice
1 teaspoon onion juice

3 hard-boiled eggs
2 tins (3¼ oz. each) sardines
  drained and boned
Tomato wedges, chopped
  parsley for garnish

Soften gelatine in ½ gill of the water. Heat remaining water to boiling point, add bouillon cubes, lemon juice, onion juice, and softened gelatine, stir until bouillon cubes and gelatine are dissolved. Pour ¼ of the gelatine mixture into a 1-quart ring mould and chill until set. Thinly slice eggs and arrange around ring mould on chilled jelly. Break sardines into short lengths and place over the eggs. Carefully spoon in remaining aspic mixture. Chill until firm. Unmould and garnish with tomato wedges dipped in chopped parsley. Makes 6 servings.

247. Whole Salmon in Aspic

1 whole salmon, about 8 lb.
Salt to taste
¼ pint water
⅓–½ lb. white-fleshed fish
1 small onion, sliced
1 sprig parsley
1 stalk celery
1 pint water
1 teaspoon salt
Dash white pepper
4 teaspoons lemon juice
1 envelope (1 tablespoon)
  unflavoured gelatine
¼ pint cold water
Pimiento strips or green pepper
  rings, sliced ripe or stuffed
  green olives

If the head is removed from the salmon, leave the collar intact. Sprinkle inside of fish with salt. Place fish on sheet of heavy foil, cup the edges, then pour in the ¼ pint water so that the salmon will steam as it cooks. Wrap foil over fish, then fold and crimp edges of foil together. Place in a shallow pan and bake in a moderate oven (350°F.) for 30 minutes or until fish will flake easily when tested with a fork. While fish is still warm, fold back foil and carefully pull off skin. Place salmon in refrigerator to chill thoroughly.

To make the aspic, combine the white fish with onion, parsley, celery, and 1 pint water. Cover and simmer gently for 25 minutes. Strain through a fine wire strainer, and measure ¾ pint of the fish stock. Add salt, pepper, and lemon juice. Meanwhile soften gelatine in the ¼ pint cold water. Bring stock to the boil, and stir in gelatine until dissolved.

Transfer the cold salmon to a serving platter and pour over a thin layer of aspic. Put back in refrigerator until aspic sets. Decorate fish with strips of pimiento or green pepper rings, and sliced ripe or green olives, dipping them into the syrupy aspic so they will stick to the fish. Pour another coat of aspic over fish and decorations. Refrigerate until decorations set in place. You might check once or twice to see that the decorations haven't slipped. Makes 12 to 15 servings.

248. Moulded Tuna Fish and Cabbage Salad

1½ gills hot water
3 oz. packaged lime jelly
¼ pint cold water
2 tablespoons vinegar
2 tablespoons lemon juice
¼ teaspoon salt

1 tin (7 oz.) tuna fish, flaked
1 cup shredded cabbage
¼ cup (4 tablespoons) chopped
 dill pickle
3 hard-boiled eggs, sliced
Crisp salad greens for garnish

Lime-flavoured jelly makes a colourful setting for layers of tuna, cabbage, pickle, and hard-boiled eggs.

Pour hot water over jelly and stir until dissolved. Stir in cold water, vinegar, lemon juice, and salt. Chill until syrupy. Arrange flaked tuna in the bottom of a 1½-quart ring mould or loaf tin. Pour one-half of the cooled jelly into the mould. Chill until firm. In the following order, arrange over the firm jelly two layers each of the cabbage, dill pickle, and egg slices. Pour over the remaining half of the jelly mixture. Chill until firm, in about 2 hours. Unmould on to a dish lined with crisp salad greens. Makes 6 servings.

249. Lemon–Lime Tuna Fish Mould

3 oz. packaged lemon jelly
3 oz. packaged lime jelly
1 pint hot water
¾ pint cold water
2 teaspoons prepared mustard
2 teaspoons lemon juice
8 level tablespoons mayonnaise
¾ cup sliced celery
1 cup cooked peas

1 tablespoon finely chopped
 onion
2 tablespoons chopped
 pimiento
2 hard-boiled eggs, coarsely
 chopped
About 14 oz. flaked tuna fish
Lettuce, radishes, and ripe
 olives for garnish

Green peas, pimiento, and chopped hard-boiled eggs are colourful spots in this pale green tuna mould. Prepared mustard and lemon juice add enough sharpness to the jelly base to keep it from being sweet.

Place jellies in a large bowl. Pour in hot water, and stir until jellies are dissolved. Stir in cold water. Chill until syrupy. Combine the mustard, lemon juice, and mayonnaise. Stir into jelly. Fold in the celery, peas, onion, pimiento, eggs, and tuna fish. Turn mixture into a 2½-quart ring mould. Chill for 3 hours, or until firm. To serve, unmould on lettuce and garnish with radishes and a few ripe olives. Makes 12 servings.

250. Crab Mousse

¾–1 lb. crab meat, flaked
3 tablespoons lemon juice
1 tablespoon sherry
1 envelope (1 tablespoon)
  unflavoured gelatine
3 tablespoons cold water
3 tablespoons chopped green
  pepper

1 cup sliced celery
1 tablespoon chopped pimiento
10 stuffed green olives, chopped
2 hard-boiled eggs, chopped
1 teaspoon salt
¼ teaspoon freshly ground pepper
½ pint whipping cream
Crisp salad greens

Fresh crab meat marinated in lemon juice and sherry adds a tang to this salad.

Mix crab meat with lemon juice and sherry and let stand. Soften gelatine in cold water and dissolve over boiling water. Stir into crab meat and lemon. Add celery, green pepper, pimiento, olives, eggs, salt, and pepper. Whip cream and fold in. Spoon into 1½-quart ring mould and chill 3 hours, or until firm. Unmould on to a bed of salad greens and fill centre of ring with pickles or a tossed green salad with a sharp dressing. Makes 6 to 8 servings.

251. Crab Meat Salad Mould

2 envelopes (2 tablespoons)
  unflavoured gelatine
¼ pint cold water
¼ pint chilli sauce or tomato
  ketchup
¼ pint whipping cream
½ pint mayonnaise
1 tablespoon lemon juice
¾ pint fresh or tinned crab meat
2 oz. grated cheese

Soften gelatine in cold water for 5 minutes. Heat chilli sauce or ketchup in double boiler. Add softened gelatine and stir until dissolved. Remove from heat and cool. Whip cream. Fold into mayonnaise, and then stir in the chilli sauce or ketchup mixture. Add lemon juice to taste. Stir in crab and grated cheese. Pour into a 2-quart ring mould and chill until firm. May be served with or without salad dressing. Makes 8 to 10 servings.

252. Moulded Avocado Ring with Seafood Salad

½ pint boiling water
3 oz. packaged lemon jelly
½ pint mayonnaise
1 tablespoon lemon juice
1 teaspoon salt
1 large avocado
½ pint whipping cream
Crisp salad greens

SEAFOOD SALAD:
1½ cups grapefruit segments
1 pint crab meat or
    shrimps
1 cup sliced celery
2 tablespoons lemon juice
3–4 tablespoons French
    dressing
¼ teaspoon celery salt

Dungeness crab and grapefruit make a colourful filling for this pale green avocado ring.

Pour boiling water over the jelly, stirring until dissolved. Cool until syrupy. Stir in the mayonnaise, lemon juice, and salt. Peel and sieve avocado (should have about ½ pint sieved pulp) and stir in. Whip cream until thick, but not stiff, and fold in. Turn into a 1 quart ring mould and chill until firm. Unmould on to a bed of crisp salad greens. Toss together lightly the grapefruit segments, crab meat, celery, lemon juice, French dressing, and celery salt. Fill centre of ring with seafood salad. Makes 8 servings.

253. Moulded Cheese Salad

1 envelope (1 tablespoon)
    unflavoured gelatine
½ gill cold water
1 tin (9 oz.) crushed
    pineapple

1 lb. ground Cheddar cheese
2–3 oz. chopped walnuts
½ pint mayonnaise
½ pint whipping cream

Use a small square of this salad as the centre of interest for a fruit plate. Surround it with pears and orange and grapefruit segments on a bed of cos lettuce.

Soften gelatine in water. Heat the pineapple. Add gelatine, and stir until dissolved. Cool. Mix in the cheese (which has been run through the medium blade of your mincer), nuts, mayonnaise, and the cream, beaten until it peaks. Turn into a deep 8-by 12-inch baking tin or two loaf tins, each 5 by 9 inches. Chill until set. Cut in squares or slice to serve. Makes 10 to 12 servings.

254. Mustard Ring

4 eggs
3– 4oz. caster sugar
1 envelope (1 tablespoon)
   unflavoured gelatine
1 tablespoon dry mustard
¼ teaspoon turmeric

¼ teaspoon salt
½ pint water
¼ pint cider vinegar
½ pint whipping cream
Salad greens

Here is an excellent salad-relish accompaniment for ham because it is
sweet, tart, colourful, and spicy, as well as attractive. For contrast to
the smooth texture of the mustard-flavoured ring mould, fill the centre
with a cabbage slaw.

Beat eggs in top of a double boiler. Mix the sugar and gelatine together
thoroughly. Stir in mustard, turmeric, and salt. Add the water and vinegar to the eggs, stir in the sugar mixture, and cook over boiling water
until slightly thickened, stirring continuously. Cool until it is thick.
Whip cream and fold in. Turn into a 1½-quart ring mould. When firm,
unmould and, if desired, fill centre with cole slaw to which you can add
frozen or tinned pineapple chunks or diced pear. Garnish with chicory,
and watercress, or other feathery greens. Makes 8 servings.

255. Egg and Onion Salad Ring

2 envelopes (2 tablespoons)
   unflavoured gelatine
½ pint cold water
9 hard-boiled eggs
½ pint mayonnaise
7 spring onions, finely sliced
1¼ teaspoons salt
Pepper to taste

¾ teaspoon Worcester sauce
½ teaspoon paprika
½ teaspoon garlic salt
1 teaspoon prepared mustard
½ cup sliced radishes
Salad greens
Thousand Island dressing
   (page 173)

For a colourful luncheon salad, you might mound cooked shrimp or
crab meat in the centre of this egg salad ring.

Sprinkle gelatine in cold water to soften. Stand 5 minutes. Place over
boiling water and stir until dissolved. Cool. Put the eggs through a sieve
or a ricer into a bowl. Stir in mayonnaise, onions, salt, pepper, Worcester
sauce, paprika, garlic salt, mustard, and radishes. Combine the egg
mixture with the cooled jelly, and turn into a greased 1½-quart ring
mould. Chill until set. Unmould on to a bed of salad greens. Serve with
Thousand Island dressing. Makes 8 servings.

256. Three-cheese Salad Mould

2 envelopes (2 tablespoons)
 unflavoured gelatine
¼ pint cold water
½ pint hot water
¼ teaspoon salt
¼ teaspoon paprika
1 tablespoon lemon juice
8 oz. cream cheese
1 oz. grated Roquefort or blue
 cheese

8 tablespoons milk
1 oz. grated Cheddar cheese
½ green pepper, seeded and
 chopped
2 tablespoons chopped pimiento
1 tablespoon finely minced
 onion (optional)
¼ pint whipping cream
Lettuce, tomato wedges, cucumber sticks for garnish

The smooth texture of this salad comes from cream cheese.

Soften gelatine in cold water. Add hot water and stir until gelatine is
dissolved. Add salt, paprika, and lemon juice. Cool. Mash cream cheese
with the Roquefort or blue cheese until mixture is blended but still
slightly lumpy. (If you prefer a more subtle Roquefort cheese flavour,
beat mixture until smooth.) Add milk and stir until well mixed. Stir in
grated cheese and cooled gelatine mixture, along with green pepper,
pimiento, and onion.

 Whip cream until thick but not stiff. Fold into cheese and gelatine
mixture. Turn into a 1½-quart ring mould and chill until firm, in about
2 hours. To serve, unmould on crisp lettuce and garnish with tomato
wedges and cucumber sticks. Makes 6 to 8 servings.

257. Tutti Frutti Salad Ring

1 envelope (1 tablespoon)
 unflavoured gelatine
3 tablespoons cold water
9 oz. mixed dried fruit
3½ gills chilled ginger ale

3 tablespoons lemon juice
3-4 tablespoons chopped nuts
Soured cream or whipped
 cream
Grated lemon peel

Unusually sweet for a jellied salad, this fruit ring is very good with cold
sliced ham or turkey.

Sprinkle gelatine into cold water. Stand 5 minutes. Chop up fruit; place
in a saucepan, and add ½ pint of the ginger ale. Bring to the boil, stirring
constantly. Boil 1 minute. Remove from heat, and stir in gelatine mixture,
lemon juice, and nuts. Stir until gelatine is dissolved. Cool. Stir in remaining ginger ale. Turn into 1½-quart ring mould. Chill at least 2 hours.
To serve, unmould and top with soured cream or whipped cream sprinkled with a little grated lemon peel. Makes 8 servings.

Salad Dressings

Salad Dressings

It is the addition of the salad dressing that always completes a salad. Therefore, be careful when balancing the quantities of the oil and vinegar, and in your choice of herbs and seasonings, when mixing your dressings. Most egg, fish, meat, and vegetable salads need a piquant dressing to pep them up. On the other hand, tart fruits take kindly to the addition of a sweet dressing, creamy if liked. A salad of crisp salad greens, or hearts or wedges of lettuce, needs an outstanding dressing to give it character.

There is no one compulsory dressing for any one salad. The choice is a matter of individual taste, but the more you vary your dressings, the more appreciated the salads will be. Flavour dressing with grated horse-radish when required to serve with boiled salt beef, roast beef, baked ham, or ox tongue. A combination of greens, tossed with a dressing seasoned with Parmesan or blue cheese, goes well with spaghetti, or any spicy dishes.

Wait until the last possible moment to add dressing to most salads, and then use just enough to accent the ingredients. When dressing is added to a tossed green salad, there should be just enough to coat all the leaves. You should not end up with a pool of dressing at the bottom of the salad bowl.

258. Tangy French Dressing

1 teaspoon salt
Dash of cayenne
¼ teaspoon pepper
½ teaspoon dry mustard
1 teaspoon Worcester sauce
1 tablespoon (or more) finely
  minced onion
1 clove garlic, finely minced
2 tablespoons vinegar
6 tablespoons salad oil

Combine all ingredients in a bowl. Beat hard with a rotary or electric beater until well blended. If dressing is not used at once, be sure to beat or shake again just before serving. Makes about ¼ pint dressing.

259. Standard French Dressing

1 teaspoon salt
1 saltspoon pepper
1 saltspoon paprika
3 tablespoons vinegar
1¼ gills salad oil

Mix the dry ingredients with the vinegar, add the oil, and beat or shake well before using. Wine vinegar, tarragon, malt, or cider vinegar may be used, or any combination of these, or lemon or grapefruit juice may replace the vinegar. Additional seasonings, such as Worcester sauce, onion, and garlic, may be added. Makes about ½ pint dressing.

260. Tomato Dressing

2 oz. caster sugar
2 teaspoons salt
1½ teaspoons dry mustard
¼ teaspoon paprika
*1 tin (10½ oz.) condensed
  tomato soup*
½ pint salad oil
1¼ gills cider vinegar
*3 tablespoons tarragon
  vinegar*
1 teaspoon Worcester sauce
1 medium-sized onion, grated
*1 clove garlic, grated or left
  whole (optional)*

Combine ingredients and beat well until the sugar is dissolved and the mixture is thick and rich. Makes about 1½ pints dressing. (This will keep indefinitely in the refrigerator.)

261. Vinaigrette Dressing

2 hard-boiled egg yolks
3 tablespoons malt vinegar
6 tablespoons salad oil
2 spring onions, chopped finely
*Salt and coarse black pepper
  to taste*

Mash yolks to a paste with vinegar. Gradually blend in oil. Add remaining ingredients and mix well. Serve with cold asparagus or broccoli, or with salad greens. Makes about 1½ gills dressing.

262. Low-calorie Dressing

½ pint cider vinegar
1 tablespoon tomato ketchup
2 tablespoons brown sugar
1 tablespoon chilli sauce
3–4 tablespoons water
½ teaspoon minced garlic
½ teaspoon dry mustard
¼ teaspoon each paprika and
*   black pepper*
1 saltspoon salt

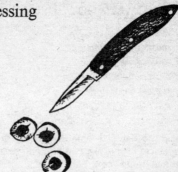

There is no oil in this salad dressing, so it should have special appeal for weight watchers.

Place all ingredients in a bowl or jar, and beat or shake well. Makes ¾–1 pint dressing.

263. Chilli Sauce Salad Dressing

2 oz. caster sugar
1 teaspoon each salt, celery seed,
*   and paprika*
½ teaspoon pepper
1 green pepper, seeded and
*   finely chopped*
1 pimiento, finely chopped
1 medium-sized onion, grated
3–4 tablespoons lemon juice
1½ gills vinegar
1 bottle (12 oz.) chilli sauce

You can toss this pimiento and green pepper-flecked salad dressing with many types of salad ingredients – mixed salad greens, mixed vegetables, crab, or shrimp.

In a 1½ quart jar with a tight-fitting cover, put the sugar, salt, celery seed, paprika, and pepper. Add the green pepper, pimiento, onion, lemon juice, vinegar, oil, and chilli sauce. Cover jar tightly and shake well. Refrigerate. Makes about 1 quart dressing.

264. Sweet–Sour Fruit Salad Dressing

1 egg
1 teaspoon salt
1 tablespoon flour
3 teaspoons caster sugar
3 tablespoons vinegar
3 tablespoons water
1 small tin (6 oz.) evaporated milk

The sweet–sour flavour of this salad dressing is a good contrast to the mildness of melons, peaches, and pears. For variety, add ½ teaspoon grated orange peel.

Beat egg together with salt, flour, and sugar in top of a double boiler. Stir in vinegar and water. Stirring constantly, cook over boiling water until smooth and slightly thick. Remove from heat and beat in evaporated milk. Store in refrigerator until required. Makes ½ pint dressing.

265. Piquant Dressing

¼ pint salad oil
3–4 tablespoons wine vinegar
3 tablespoons dry white table
  wine
1 teaspoon Worcester sauce
3 or 4 drops Tabasco
1 tablespoon brown sugar
1 teaspoon salt
1 teaspoon paprika
¼ teaspoon coarse black pepper
1 clove garlic, peeled

This light dressing goes well with most green salads. It's our first choice for the Green Salad, Smörgåsbord Style. (Recipe 1)

Combine all the ingredients in a covered pint jar. Shake until very well blended. Set aside several hours or overnight before using. Discard garlic. Makes ¾ pint dressing.

266. Caesar Style Dressing

1¼ gills salad oil
3 tablespoons lime or lemon
juice
4 tablespoons grated Parmesan
cheese
2 tablespoons finely chopped
spring onion
1 teaspoon salt
¾ teaspoon dry mustard
½ teaspoon garlic salt
¼ teaspoon coarse black pepper
¼ teaspoon Worcester or soy
sauce

This is a modified Caesar dressing. You can make it up early to toss with torn cos lettuce leaves. It contains no raw egg, yet retains the characteristic flavour of true Caesar dressing. It has a particularly good clinging quality. Bits of cheese nestle in the dips of the leaves.

Combine all ingredients in a covered jar and shake thoroughly. Chill. Shake again before using. Makes about ¾ pint dressing.

267. Minced Vegetable Salad Dressing

1 medium-sized onion
1 tin (4 oz.) pimientos
1 large green pepper
½ pint salad oil
Caster sugar to taste
1 dessertspoon salt
1¼ gills vinegar

Use this colourful dressing on wedges of lettuce or over a salad of mixed raw and cooked vegetables.

Run the onion, pimientos, and seeded green pepper through the medium blade of your mincer. Put ground vegetables in a quart jar. Add oil, sugar, salt, and vinegar. Shake well. Store in the refrigerator. Shake again each time you use it. Makes about 1 quart of dressing.

268. Celery Seed Salad Dressing

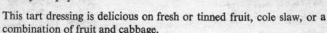

1 oz. caster sugar
1 teaspoon salt
½ teaspoon dry mustard
1 teaspoon onion juice
3 tablespoons cider vinegar
½ pint salad oil
1 to 1½ teaspoons celery seeds
1 teaspoon paprika

This tart dressing is delicious on fresh or tinned fruit, cole slaw, or a combination of fruit and cabbage.

Combine sugar, salt, mustard, onion juice, vinegar, salad oil, celery seeds, and paprika in a small bowl and beat well. Chill well before serving. Makes about 2½ gills dressing.

269. American Papaya Seed Dressing

6 oz. caster sugar
1 teaspoon salt
1 teaspoon dry mustard
½ pint wine vinegar
1 pint salad oil
1 small onion
1 tablespoon papaya seeds

Serve this dressing on fruit salads, such as the fruit plate of papaya, orange, banana, and pineapple slices pictured on Plate 14a.

Mix sugar, salt, mustard, and vinegar. Add oil gradually, beating constantly. Grate onion. Add along with papaya seeds. Stir to blend well. If dressing separates on standing, whip it up again before serving. Makes 1½ pints dressing.

270. Roquefort French Dressing

Combine 2 tablespoons crumbled Roquefort cheese and ¼ pint French dressing. Shake or stir well before serving. Serve with any crisp green salad.

271. Barbara Worth Salad Dressing

1 large clove garlic
1 teaspoon salt
½ pint olive or salad oil
¼ pint red wine vinegar
¼ pint whipping cream
1 tablespoon sesame seeds
Freshly ground black pepper
   to taste

Dice garlic on a chopping board. Sprinkle with salt, then work salt and garlic together, using the flat blade of a table knife, until garlic is completely blended with salt. Combine with remaining ingredients. Stir well or shake in a jar. Allow dressing to ripen for several hours, and stir or shake well just before using. Makes about 1½ pints dressing.

NOTE : If sesame seeds are not available substitute caraway.

272. Thousand Island Dressing

½ pint mayonnaise
2 tablespoons chilli sauce
1 tablespoon chopped sweet
   pickle
2 tablespoons chopped stuffed
   olives
1 hard-boiled egg, chopped
   finely
½ teaspoon grated onion
¼ pint whipped cream or ½ gill
   French dressing

Mix ingredients in the order given and chill thoroughly before serving. Serve with vegetable salads. Makes about 1 pint dressing.

273. Russian Dressing

To ½ pint mayonnaise, add 2 tablespoons each chilli sauce and finely chopped pimiento or green pepper, and ½ teaspoon each vinegar and paprika. Mix well. Half a hard-boiled egg, chopped finely, and 1 tablespoon chopped chives may also be added. Delicious with green, vegetable, egg, or fish salads. Makes about ¾ pint dressing.

274. American Poppy Seed Dressing

Caster sugar to taste
1 teaspoon dry mustard
1 teaspoon salt
4 tablespoons cider vinegar
½ pint salad oil
1 tablespoon very finely minced
   onion
1 teaspoon each poppy seeds
   and caraway seeds

This sweet American dressing with crunchy black poppy seeds and caraway seeds is sometimes served in the United States with fruit salads. The amount of sugar used can vary from 3 to 5 oz.

Sift sugar, mustard, and salt together into a bowl. Blend in vinegar. With a rotary beater, gradually beat in oil. Stir in onion, poppy seeds, and caraway seeds. Chill thoroughly in a quart jar. Shake well before serving over any fruit salad. Makes ¾ pint dressing.

275. Mayonnaise

2 egg yolks
1 teaspoon salt
1 teaspoon caster sugar
   (optional)
1 teaspoon dry mustard
Dash of cayenne
2 to 4 tablespoons lemon juice
   or vinegar
3½ gills salad oil

In a deep bowl, thoroughly mix the egg yolks with salt, sugar, mustard, and cayenne. Stir in 2 tablespoons lemon juice or vinegar. While beating briskly with a rotary beater, start adding the oil, a few drops at a time. Beat well after each addition until about ¼ pint of the oil has been added. Beat in the remaining oil, adding it about 2 tablespoons at a time. Makes about 1–1¼ pints dressing.

276. Caviar Mayonnaise

Gently mix together ½ pint mayonnaise, 3 to 4 tablespoons red caviar, 1 tablespoon lemon juice, and 1 teaspoon grated onion. Use in place of plain mayonnaise with any fish salad, or toss with chilled, crisp salad greens. If necessary, thin the dressing with a little cream so that it will mingle more readily with the greens. You might also use this as a dip for prawns, potato chips or puffs, cauliflower sprigs, etc.

277. Watercress Salad Dressing

½ bunch watercress
1 clove garlic, minced or
*   mashed*
½ pint mayonnaise
Salt to taste
2 teaspoons lemon juice

In this mayonnaise dressing, watercress provides a spicy flavour and a bright green colour. For a time-saver, put all ingredients in your blender and blend just until watercress is finely minced.
Chop watercress and garlic very finely. Stir into mayonnaise. Add salt to taste and lemon juice. Chill. Serve over lettuce or a salad of orange and grapefruit segments. Makes about ¾ pint of dressing.

278. Cucumber Salad Dressing

½ pint shredded cucumber, drained
1½ gills mayonnaise
¼ teaspoon crushed herbs
2 spring onions, finely minced
2 teaspoons red wine vinegar
1 saltspoon basil
¼ teaspoon salt

Mix cucumber with mayonnaise. Stir in remaining ingredients and chill until required. Makes about ¾ pint dressing.

279. Honey Lime Dressing

Juice of 2 large fresh limes
2 tablespoons light, mild honey
1½ gills salad oil
1 saltspoon salt

Honey sweetens this salad dressing made with lime juice. It is particularly good on a fruit, melon, or lettuce salad. It's best to make up only a small quantity of this dressing at one time so the lime doesn't lose its fresh flavour.

Strain lime juice and blend in honey. Add oil and salt and pour into a jar or covered plastic container. Shake well. Store in refrigerator. Shake again before using. Makes about ½ pint dressing.

280. Fruit Salad Dressing

2 tablespoons lemon juice
¼ pint fresh or frozen orange juice
¼ pint fresh or tinned pineapple juice
Pinch of salt
1 tablespoon maraschino cherry juice
3 tablespoons honey
1 tablespoon cornflour
¼ teaspoon celery seeds
¼ teaspoon minced parsley

The tartness of the lemon, orange, and pineapple juice makes this an ideal dressing for both fresh and tinned fruits. For a richer dressing, blend in an equal amount of whipped cream.

Blend the lemon, orange, and pineapple juices with salt, cherry juice, honey, and cornflour in top of double boiler. Cook over hot water until thickened, stirring constantly. Stir in the celery seeds and parsley, and chill. Makes about ¾ pint dressing. Toss with desired fruits, or serve separately.

281. Creamy Banana Dressing

2 medium-sized ripe peeled
   bananas
3–4 tablespoons mayonnaise
3–4 tablespoons buttermilk
3 tablespoons lemon juice
2 teaspoons grated horseradish
¼ teaspoon salt
1 teaspoon caster sugar
¼ teaspoon Tabasco

Here's a delicious dressing for cabbage slaw, especially those combinations that include fruit. Try it on a salad made of finely shredded cabbage with seeded grapes and a few chopped nuts.

Using a blender, whip together bananas, mayonnaise, buttermilk, lemon juice, horseradish, salt, sugar, and Tabasco. If you don't have a blender, use your electric mixer or a rotary egg-beater to beat the ingredients together until smooth. Makes about 1 pint dressing.

282. Sour Cream Dressing

2–3 oz. caster sugar
Salt to taste
¼ teaspoon white pepper
2 teaspoons prepared mustard
3 tablespoons flour

3½ gills soured cream
1½ gills strained lemon juice
3 tablespoons water
Whipped cream as required

You may serve this dressing either cold or hot. When you use it cold with shredded cabbage or fruit, thin it with whipped cream. When you wish it hot, simply reheat and mix immediately with potatoes, cabbage, or salad greens.

Blend sugar, salt, pepper, mustard, and flour together in the top of a double boiler. Gradually add soured cream, stirring constantly. Combine lemon juice and water and pour in. Cook over boiling water, stirring constantly, until thick and smooth. Remove from heat. Stir occasionally while cooling to prevent a film from forming. Store in a covered container in refrigerator. Thin with whipped cream to desired consistency before serving. Makes about 1½ pints dressing.

283. Creamy Dressing for Moulded Salads

2 large eggs
¼ pint honey
Juice of 1 lime or lemon
¼ pint whipping cream

A fluffy, not too sweet, dressing that is best with moulded fruit or dessert salads. It should be served the same day it is made. The type of honey used will determine the flavour of the dressing.

Beat eggs until light. Stir in honey and lemon or lime juice. Cook over boiling water until thick, stirring constantly. Then cool. Whip cream until stiff and fold into honey mixture. Chill at least 1 hour before serving. Makes enough for 8 salads.

284. Anchovy Sour Cream Salad Dressing

3 hard-boiled eggs
1 bunch spring onions
1 clove garlic
2 oz. anchovy fillets
2 tablespoons mayonnaise
1 tablespoon vinegar
¼ pint soured cream
Few drops of Tabasco

Finely chop eggs, onions (tops and all), garlic, and anchovy fillets. Stir in mayonnaise, vinegar, soured cream, and Tabasco. Chill for several hours before using for dressing fish or vegetable salads. Makes about ¾ pint dressing.

285. Date Sour Cream Dressing

8 oz. stoned dates
¼ pint water
¼ pint soured cream

Combine this creamy sweet dressing with sliced fresh fruits or crisp chopped apples and celery for a salad of surprising character.

Bring dates and water to the boil and simmer 10 minutes. Cool. Chop dates very finely. Blend dates and soured cream thoroughly with a fork or rotary beater. Makes ¾ pint dressing.

286. Marshmallow Dressing

12 marshmallows
1 egg
1 tablespoon lemon juice
¼ tablespoon caster sugar
1 teaspoon salt
¼ pint whipping cream

Dissolve marshmallows by heating in the top of double boiler over hot water, stirring occasionally. Beat egg, stir in lemon juice, sugar, and salt. Add to marshmallows. Cook 2 minutes, or until mixture thickens, stirring constantly. Cool. Whip cream and fold into cold mixture. Serve over fruit or moulded salads. Makes enough for 8 salads.

287. Mint Cream Dressing

4 oz. curd cottage cheese
1 tablespoon mint jelly
Grated peel and juice of 1 lime
3 tablespoons orange juice

Whirl cottage cheese, jelly, lime peel, lime juice, and orange juice in a blender until smooth, or force through a fine wire strainer several times. Spoon over your favourite sliced fruits. Makes 1½ gills dressing.

288. Apricot Cream Dressing

3 oz. cream cheese
¼ pint apricot nectar
1 tablespoon lemon juice
3 tablespoons mayonnaise
Dash of salt

Apricot nectar gives this cream cheese dressing a tangy flavour. Serve it over a mixed fruit salad. If preferred, substitute thick cream for mayonnaise.

Soften cream cheese with a fork. Blend in apricot nectar and beat until smooth. Add the lemon juice, mayonnaise, and salt, and mix well. Makes about ½ pint dressing.

289. Cottage Cheese Salad Dressing

8 oz. large curd
cottage cheese
3 tablespoons French dressing
3 tablespoons vinegar
1 tablespoon grated Parmesan
cheese
¼ teaspoon garlic purée or 1
clove garlic, mashed
¼ teaspoon each salt and pepper

The base of this low-calorie dressing is cottage cheese. Garlic and Parmesan cheese make it pungent.

In a mixing bowl, combine the cottage cheese, French dressing, vinegar, Parmesan cheese, garlic, salt, and pepper, and beat with a rotary beater until smooth and creamy. Makes ¾ pint dressing.

290. Creamy Cheese–Avocado Dressing

1 medium-sized ripe
avocado
3–4 tablespoons soured cream
2 tablespoons finely minced
spring onion
1 tablespoon lime or lemon juice
¼ teaspoon each salt, garlic salt,
and Worcester sauce
3 tablespoons crumbled Roquefort
cheese
1½ gills salad oil
3 tablespoons each dry white
wine and wine vinegar

Peel and remove stone from avocado. Mash fruit until very smooth. Blend in soured cream, onion, lime juice, salt, garlic salt, and Worcester sauce. Mash cheese until almost smooth; blend in oil, wine, and vinegar. Combine with avocado mixture. Chill well. Makes about 1½ pints dressing.

291. Roquefort Cheese Dressing

*About 3¼ gills olive or other
    salad oil*
4 cloves garlic
4 oz. Roquefort or blue cheese
3 tablespoons vinegar
1 tablespoon caster sugar
1 tablespoon salt
¼ teaspoon pepper
4 or 5 drops Worcester sauce

This Roquefort cheese dressing has been created for mixing in an electric blender.

Add a small amount of oil to the garlic in the blender, and blend at high speed to mix well. Add about half the cheese and blend for a short time. Then add enough more oil to make 1 pint of dressing. (Add oil in small amounts, blending well after each addition.) Mix the rest of the cheese with remaining ingredients. Place in the refrigerator for several hours or overnight. Makes about 1½ pints dressing.

292. Three-cheese Dressing

¼ lb. blue cheese
8 oz. cream cheese
4 tablespoons grated sage cheese
¼ teaspoon chopped tarragon
1 teaspoon salt
¼ teaspoon pepper
¼ clove garlic, mashed
About ¼ pint milk

This blue cheese dressing has an intriguing extra flavour contributed by sage cheese. The cream cheese blends the ingredients into a smooth dressing that is delicious on tossed green salads and other vegetable salads.

Using the small bowl of your electric mixer, mix together the blue cheese, cream cheese, and sage cheese until well blended. Add the tarragon, salt, pepper, and garlic purée. Gradually beat in milk until the dressing is the consistency of medium-thick cream. Use immediately, or cover and refrigerate to use later. Makes about 1½ pints dressing.

Glossary and Index

Glossary

BOLOGNA: A large smoked Italian sausage, made of bacon, veal, and pork.

CHERRY TOMATOES: A small variety of tomatoes.

ESCAROLE: Sometimes known as a Batavian lettuce. Somewhat like curly endive, but with broad leaves. Any lettuce can be substituted in recipes including escarole.

GARBANZOS: Also known as chick peas. Sold in Continental stores, also in tins. If not available substitute tinned peas.

ICEBERG LETTUCE: Crisp, crunchy lettuce with leaves folding over each other to form a heart. When not available, substitute Webb's Wonder.

KOHL-RABI: Sometimes called a 'cabbage-turnip'. A species of cabbage. When not available, substitute small turnips.

KUMQUATS: Small citrus fruit. Grown chiefly in China and Japan. Rarely exported except tinned or preserved. Substitute mandarins.

MANGOES: A tropical fruit about the size of a large pear. If not available, substitute pears.

OREGANO: Herb somewhat similar to thyme, but more delicate in flavour. When not available, substitute a smaller quantity of thyme or marjoram.

PAPAYA: A South American fruit similar to melon. Sometimes called pawpaw. When not available substitute melon.

PECANS: Richly flavoured nuts, somewhat like walnuts.

SESAME SEEDS: Substitute caraway seeds.

WATER CHESTNUTS: Sold in tins, where Chinese foods are stocked.

ZUCCHINI: Frequently sold as 'courgettes'. Small cucumber-shaped Italian marrow.

Index

References are to recipe numbers, except where otherwise stated

*Photographs in this book by: Clyde Childress, Glen Christiansen, Robert Cox,
Blair Stapp, Darrow Watt*